MODERN MUSIC

THOMAS Y. CROWELL COMPANY   NEW YORK

MODERN

A POPULAR GUIDE TO GREATER MUSICAL ENJOYMENT

MUSIC

by John Tasker Howard and James Lyons

REVISED EDITION

BY JOHN TASKER HOWARD

Our American Music

A Program Outline of American Music

Ethelbert Nevin

Stephen Foster, America's Troubadour

Our Contemporary Composers

Modern Music (with James Lyons)

Designed by EMIL SILVESTRI

LIBRARY OF CONGRESS CATALOG CARD NO. 57-6564

Fourth Printing (First Printing of Revised Edition), April 1957

CONTENTS

WHAT IS MODERN MUSIC—
AND WHY HAVE PEOPLE NEVER
LIKED IT, AT FIRST?

THE WORD "MODERN" IS A MOST IMPERMANENT ADJECTIVE.
If it means something that belongs exclusively to present
or recent times it cannot be used for anything that was
modern a few years ago. Long-distance dialing was certainly
modern in 1956, but the telephone itself, newfangled in
1900, is hardly considered modern by the younger generation of mid-century, even though some of us who witnessed
its introduction still think of it as a modern means of com-
munication.

In the arts modernism is a particularly impermanent term,
often inaccurate for what may have been truly modern a
quarter-century ago. It does not require much of a memory
to recall the days when subscribers who had already paid for
their tickets refused to attend concerts at which *Till Eulenspiegel* was to be played.

Also, the degree of modernism in music and painting depends on the experience and taste of those who listen to
symphonies and look at pictures. To some Debussy is still
a modernist. To others Stravinsky's *Fire Bird* and even the
Rite of Spring are no longer modern and have become "old
hat." Thus the significance of the term depends on the point
of view of the individual listener, on whether he has become
accustomed to more recent patterns or whether he has ex-
posed himself so infrequently to the works of the past half-
century that he still considers the composers of the nine-

teenth century as the norm and standard of all music—past
or present.

Apart from the individual listener's conception of modernism it is essential that the term be defined for purposes of
discussion in this volume. If we accept the dictionary definition of the modern as that which originates in the present we
shall become hopelessly confused with what is merely contemporary, for if we consider as modern anything and everything that is written in present times we shall find that we
have many works which in style and idiom belong in the past.

Therefore, to be modern a composition must have other
qualities than newness alone; it must deviate in varying degree from tradition in its material and in its style. Further-
more, much of it will have experienced opposition to what
Ernst Křenek once called its "conversion into merchandise."
It will have been resisted by the public and have found acceptance by concert artists and commercial publishers difficult.

Obviously, this volume will consider as modern only that
music which when it was created departed from previous
convention and was not readily accepted. We are not concerned with music that is old-fashioned and conventional
in style even though it was composed as recently as last
month. And since the term is relative we shall have to consider the modern music of various periods in history. Mozart
wrote modern music in the latter eighteenth century, so we
are concerned with Mozart's music. John Smith in the middle
of the twentieth century writes music that Mozart might
have written, so we shall not bother our heads with it.

It is interesting to find how the lay public, and musicians
too, have reacted to the modern music of their time. Generally they have taken a rather dim view of it, which is not
altogether surprising. Our ancestors didn't like it either,
even though their modern music was written by Monteverdi,

Mozart, Beethoven, and Wagner. Human beings are by nature too complacent to like violent changes, and older generations have always lamented the passing of the "good old days." Even the most adventurous pioneers have taken with them as much of their home environment as they could carry, and as soon as they have made a permanent settlement they have re-created as much of the atmosphere of their former homes as the geography and climate of their new surroundings would permit. Thus, we find New England architecture in Ohio, Spanish buildings in California, and Chinatowns in San Francisco and New York.

If venturesome emigrants demand familiar surroundings, what about those of us who stay at home, among the same neighbors, working at the same jobs, playing the same old games? Fashion designers may create radical changes from season to season to force people to buy new clothes, but most husbands resent the way their wives look in their new hats as much as they are annoyed by the bills. And if anything so trivial as a new set of contract bridge conventions is upsetting to our peace of mind, is it any wonder that new political and sociological ideas give everyone the jitters?

Most of us admit that the world is changing: socially, economically, and politically, so whether we like it or not, we know that our mode of life will have to be adapted to the world about us. Yet, while we are broadminded and practical enough to accomplish this growth in the major matters of life, it seems to some of us a bit futile and unnecessary to disturb ourselves with changes in the less vital things, among them, music.

Music, however, is a living language; or rather, *good* music is. It is composed by human beings, and human beings do have to adapt themselves to shifting conditions, no matter how much they resist them at first. Hence, if music is to remain a living language, that is, if it is to be a sincere and honest expression of the men and women who compose it, it too must grow. Like all languages, it must constantly acquire new words and expressions to convey its meaning in a changing society.

The same principle is true of any language. Greek and Latin are dead languages because they are not used any more for daily conversation; they belonged to past civilizations and have not been adapted to more recent affairs. There are no Greek and Latin words for oil burner, cocktail, movies, television, or jet planes. The dictionaries and grammars of living languages—modern Greek and Italian, English, French, German—are continually revised and brought up to date by the inclusion of new words, and of new phrases and sentence constructions formerly considered bad usage.

It is because music is a living language that we have the so-called modern music. Music is a medium that is constantly increasing its vocabulary and taking into its grammar various devices of harmony, melody, and rhythm that were formerly forbidden by rule. If it failed to accomplish such changes it would soon be as dead as Greek and Latin, and interesting chiefly to historians.

It may be that the music of our day is far more radical, and breaks more sharply with tradition, than did the new music of Mozart, Beethoven, or Mendelssohn, but the conservative music lovers of those days thought their new music shocking enough. Go back even further, to the sixteenth century, and you find Claudio Monteverdi causing as much furor by championing the major-minor tonal system as Schoenberg has caused in our time with his atonality. In the year 1600 a critic wrote of Monteverdi: "Though I am glad of a new manner of composition, it would be more edifying to find in these madrigals reasonable passages, but these kinds of air-castles and chimeras deserve the severest reproof. . . . You hear a medley of sounds, a variety of parts that are intolerable to the ear. . . . With all the best will in the world, how can the mind see light in this chaos?"

Not many of us today would think of Mozart as a disconcerting modernist, but read what an eighteenth-century critic thought of his latest string quartets: "It is a pity that in his truly artistic and beautiful compositions Mozart should carry his effort after originality too far, to the detriment of the sentiment and heart of his works. His new quartets . . . are much too highly spiced to be palatable for any length of time."

A Vienna music patron had several of these quartets performed at his home, and was so enraged at finding the dissonances in one of them actually printed in the music that he tore the parts to pieces. Haydn, however, remarked that if Mozart wrote his music with dissonances, he must have had good reasons for doing so.

Beethoven was a shocking radical. He opened his C major symphony, the First, with a chord from the key of F, and passed through the key of G before getting down to business in C, the ruling key of the symphony. At one point in his Third Symphony, the *Eroica,* he had two different chords sounded at the same time. A contemporary critic explained this by saying that "poor Beethoven is so deaf that he cannot hear the discords he writes." One conductor went so far as to correct the "error" at rehearsal.

The composers of the romantic movement—Chopin, Mendelssohn, Schubert, Schumann, Brahms, Wagner—were all resisted by the conservatives and reactionaries of their time. Robert Schumann's teacher never forgave him for admiring Chopin, and when Schumann championed the young Brahms, he was a lone prophet crying in a classic wilderness.

Music is almost always an expression of the age in which it is written. If it isn't, we may be sure that the composer himself belongs spiritually to another age, or that he patterns his work after the music of earlier composers, unconsciously or perhaps deliberately. Then we say that his style is Wagnerian, or Franckian, instead of John Smithian.

This does not mean that originality alone is a sign of greatness, or even a virtue in itself. Progress and change are by no means synonymous. Many things may be wholly original and yet be altogether worthless, and it must be admitted that some composers sacrifice a great deal for what they believe to be originality. It seems as though their chief concern is to keep their music from bearing even the slightest resemblance to anything that has been written before. In such cases, the composer is substituting for sincere expression a conscious style which will inevitably prove artificial and manufactured. If he announces that he never listens to other men's works for fear it will destroy his individuality, he is explaining the limitations of his own music.

The casual listener to music, in the concert hall or on the radio and phonograph, may wonder how he can possibly distinguish between the genuine article and the work of a charlatan. How, for example, is the man to whom the connecting links of a Beethoven symphony are still a mystery, to know whether Stravinsky's *Rite of Spring* is an authentic art expression, which he ought to like, or merely a confusion of shocking, ugly sounds? And how is he to acquire the ability to enjoy anything that is at first hearing so highly unpleasant to his ears and his nervous system? Why torture himself by listening to it?

These are the questions this book will try to answer. The music lover must make up his mind that he is going to hear a great deal of modern music if he goes to concerts, or listens to all the numbers on a radio or TV program. If he buys tickets to hear a Beethoven symphony, he may have to listen first to a ballet suite by Stravinsky. Even if he is willing to come late and miss half of what he is paying for, his wife, or whomever he is taking to the concert, may like Stravinsky, and insist that they hear the entire program.

He needn't feel too badly if he thinks the whole business a terrible mess. If the new music is being played for the first time, he will no doubt have plenty of company in his opinion among the professional critics. And he has a distinct advantage over the critics; he may express his opinions to any or all of his friends, and suffer no ill consequences. He has little to lose if the ensuing years prove him wrong. The critic, however, must go on record in print, and allow historians of the future to dig in the files and show him up to posterity.

And how often these unfortunate gentlemen have turned out to be wrong, down through the history of music right to the present day! Gounod once remarked that César Franck's Symphony in D Minor represented the height of incompetence carried to dogmatic lengths, while in 1905 Richard Aldrich in *The New York Times* described Rimsky-Korsakov's *Scheherazade* as "dull," with an "insistence on long drawn oriental chantings and dronings."

The following paragraph might well describe the worthless product of a third- or fourth-rate composition student:

"Last night's concert began with a lot of impressionistic daubs of color smeared higgledy-piggledy on a tonal palette, with never a thought of form or purpose except to create new combinations of sounds. . . . One thing only was certain, and that was that the composer's ocean was a frog-pond, and that some of its denizens had got into the throat of every one of the brass instruments."

Those words were written in 1907 for the New York *Tribune*, by Henry E. Krehbiel, one of the soundest and most learned critics who has ever written for a metropolitan

journal, and the work he described was Debussy's *La Mer*
Fifteen years later Krehbiel again reviewed a performance
of *La Mer*, and called it a "poetic work in which Debussy
has so wondrously caught the rhythms and colors of the seas."

The inference to be drawn from these two opinions is
clear. When Krehbiel first heard *La Mer*, its strangeness confused him. Fifteen years later he had absorbed the idiom,
and become so familiar with it that it had ceased to bother
him, and he was able to grasp the true beauty of the work.

Read also what Krehbiel wrote about the Fourth Symphony of Tchaikovsky when he first heard it, in 1890:

"Of the four symphonies of Tchaikovsky which have been
heard in New York, it is far and away the least interesting.
It is the first of the larger works of the genial Russian, con-
cerning which we feel tempted to say that it ought not to
have been performed at all. It would have been treated with
manifest kindness if its *Scherzo* had been incorporated in
the scheme of some popular concert and the rest of it had
been consigned to the limbo of oblivion. The *Scherzo* utilizes
the strings *pizzicato* throughout and is pretty. Artistically,
it stands on the plane, say, of Strauss's *Pizzicato Polka*,
though not quite as graceful. As a symphonic movement,
it is about as dignified as one of the compositions which
delight the souls of college banjo clubs. But in spite of the
striving evidenced by Tchaikovsky's recurrence in his last
movement to material used in the *Introduction* and the first
movement . . . the composition can scarcely be called a
Symphony, except on the principle of *lucus a non lucendo*.
It wants nearly every element which makes the work which
opened the concert, for instance [Mozart's G minor], a symphony. There was a great show of effort in the composition,
but only a modicum of artistic result."

Again, the critic resisted something new. The first three symphonies of Tchaikovsky were conventional and, incidentally, are rarely if ever heard today. In the Fourth, Tchaikovsky ventured in new fields. He extended the traditional forms, and used a Russian folk song as a motto that tied the work together by recurring in the last movement. Krehbiel didn't like it; its novelty was so offensive to him that he missed entirely the power and dramatic force that have come to thrill thousands, perhaps millions, of music lovers.

Resistance to new music has always existed to a certain degree, particularly on the part of critics, but it is only in the last century and a half that it has become a violent and hostile public reaction. It was in the nineteenth century that the worship of the "old masters" came into being, with its establishment of a standard repertory for symphony orchestras and for individual concert artists. Nowadays new music is played by major organizations largely for general prestige, as a contribution to the advancement of music, not as an immediate box-office attraction. Concert artists look for cash customers for Beethoven, Wagner, or Tchaikovsky; not for the new and untried.

In the seventeen hundreds the situation was considerably different. The repertory had not yet come into existence, and new works were performed more often than old ones. Some of this may be explained by the fact that music was still largely the diversion of kings and princes, who maintained their own musicians to perform for the court. It was the duty of the *Kapellmeister* to engage and train the musicians of the court. Music to play was needed, of course, and generally the *Kapellmeister*, in his own handwriting, would arrange and adapt the parts for performance as an incidental part of his duties. He was expected to compose music of his own for all occasions, and even when he played other men's music, it was generally new. Thus, Prince Esterházy required Haydn to keep his private orchestra supplied with new symphonies, and his quartet with new chamber music.

At the Thomaskirche in Leipzig, Bach was expected to write a new cantata each week, and his large family was kept busy copying out the parts as the father finished each page of the score. During the several years that Bach was *Kapellmeister* for Prince Leopold at Köthen, he wrote the bulk of his orchestral and chamber music. But this was for performance by the Prince's musicians, not for publication. It was not until years later that these works were published and available for performance elsewhere.

When concerts for the public became regular features of European cities, particularly in England, the people apparently wanted new music at first, for the eighteenth-century newspaper announcements invariably featured new works. When Haydn went to London, the contract called for twelve new symphonies to be played at his concerts—six on each visit. There was also a demand from the British public for a constant supply of new operas, oratorios, and instrumental works by Handel. In 1742 the Dublin papers announced that "on Monday, the 12th of April, for the benefit of the Prisoners of the several Gaols, and the support of Mercer's Hospital, in Stephen's-street, and of the Charitable Infirmary on the Inn's Quay, will be performed at the Musick Hall in Fishambe-street, Mr. Handel's *new Grand Oratorio, called the Messiah,* in which the Gentlemen of the Choirs of both Cathedrals will assist, with some Concertos on the Organ, by Mr. Handell."

It was the same in America. When George Washington visited Boston, a few months after his inauguration as president, a huge concert was planned in his honor. The newspapers announced that the program would contain the "Oratorio of *Jonah*, which has been applauded by the best judges and has never been performed in America." Again in Boston, a Mr. Turner advertised a concert in 1773, and respectfully begged leave "to acquaint his subscribers that his last concert for the season will be on Tues. eve, at which time will be performed a variety of music received from London by Capt. Scott, which never has been performed in this place."

All of this was in the eighteenth century. In the nineteenth century, concerts and opera became the diversion of the people, not alone the luxury of aristocrats. With the public demand for the familiar, there came a resistance to new music that made it difficult for young revolutionary composers to gain a sympathetic hearing. As Ernst Křenek has written: "Theaters and concert halls were thrown open to an enormously increasing number of people, and the operation of music as an institution had thenceforth to depend for its sustenance upon this new audience's desire to buy and its power to buy, a service which formerly was essentially performed by small privileged groups." [1] Thus, in our own time, we find that radical new music generally has its first hearing at nonprofit-making concerts sponsored by groups of composers or subsidized by philanthropists.

The inexperienced layman, then, is not alone in his disinclination to bother himself with listening to modern music. Sometimes, however, he is more receptive to it than professionals are, for though he may like best the things he is familiar with, he is often far less hemmed in by traditions than is the veteran concert-goer. Virgil Thomson has gone so far as to claim that modern music is easier for the layman to understand than old music. In an article on "Understanding Modern Music" he wrote:

[1] *Music Here and Now.* New York: W. W. Norton & Co., Inc., 1939.

"There is no reason why anybody in the music world, professional or layman, should find himself in the position of not understanding a piece of twentieth-century music, if he is willing to give himself a little trouble. . . . The art-music of the past, most of all that eighteenth and nineteenth century repertory known as 'classical' music, is, on the other hand, about as incomprehensible as anything could be. Its idiom is comprehensible, because it is familiar. But its significant content is as impenetrable as that of the art work of the Middle Ages. It was made by men whose modes of thought and attitudes of passion were as different from ours as those of Voltaire and Goethe and Rousseau . . . were different from those of Bernard Shaw . . . and Gertrude Stein and Mickey Mouse. . . ." [2]

It is surely too much to say that a twentieth-century listener cannot penetrate to the spiritual content of Beethoven, but Mr. Thomson was sound in stating that, aside from the idiom of a contemporary work, no listener can fail to penetrate its meaning, at least partially.

The listener's problem is one of understanding something of the composer's method, and of how his style differs from that of composers in the past. Then he can decide for himself whether or not the twentieth-century message is coherently and effectively expressed; in other words, he will know whether or not he is likely to enjoy a new composition when he has become used to its style and mode of expression.

If he is a lover of the classics, if he likes to listen to his "old favorites," he must realize why music must change its style with the centuries. In the next chapter we shall find how music expresses and reflects the background of the age in which it was composed. Thus, in the twentieth century, when a composer writes descriptive music, he will deal with

[2] New York *Herald Tribune*, Jan. 4, 1942.

the sights and sounds that belong to his own era, and instead of painting tone-pictures of sailing vessels he will depict the speedier ocean liners and jet planes; instead of blacksmith shops, he will paint steel mills. In drawing his musical scenes, he finds that the melodic, rhythmic, and harmonic vocabulary of Beethoven will not suffice for the mighty roar of the plunging giant of steel, and like Honegger in *Pacific 231*, he will draw on new combinations of sounds to sing the song of the great locomotive. Nor will the chastely simple pattern of Handel's *Harmonious Blacksmith* serve for describing an iron foundry. The crude dissonances of Mossolov's *Soviet Iron Foundry* are less tuneful, but more faithful to their subject.

Entirely apart from the descriptive functions of music, how can we expect the musical speech of Handel to express the restless, uncertain temper of our age any more effectively than the literary style of *Godey's Lady's Book* would describe an air raid in the pages of *Life* or *Time*? The march of science, the invention of machines, have created an atmosphere wholly unlike the environment that surrounded our fathers.

We need music that expresses the way we feel in our own age. It is not sound to say that we have enough music already, for there must be music to express the voice of every age. If the music lovers of Mozart's day had refused altogether to listen to new music, we wouldn't have any Beethoven. And if the concert-goers of Beethoven's day had decided that they had enough music (which some of them almost did), then there would have been no Schumann, Mendelssohn, Wagner, or Brahms.

For unless we listen to our new music, it will not exist. When music is not performed, it is merely a set of symbols on paper. None of us can tell who the Mozarts or the Beethovens of the future will be, but we must make sure that

when they come, if they are not here already, they will have
a chance to be heard.

There are just two things that the music lover who wants
to enjoy modern music need do. First, he must realize *why*
it is what it is; why the composers of every age have written
differently from those who preceded them. Secondly, he
must acquaint himself, if only superficially, with a few of the
methods used by modern composers to make their music
different from eighteenth- and nineteenth-century music.
Then he will know whether they have used their tools and
materials effectively or inefficiently. And he may come to
have a fair idea as to which of them are creative artists and
which are mountebanks and fakers.

2 MUSIC HAS ALWAYS TOLD HOW PEOPLE THINK AND ACT

PLATO WAS SOMETHING OF A PROPHET WHEN HE WROTE THAT the introduction of a new style of music must be shunned as imperiling the whole state, since styles of music are never disturbed without affecting the most important institutions. "The new style," he explained, "quietly insinuates itself into manners and customs, and from these it issues a greater force . . . goes on to attack laws and constitutions, displaying the utmost impudence, until it ends by overturning everything, both in public and in private."

He might almost have been writing about the "rock and roll" riots of 1956, and, if he were living in our age, arguing that jazz and swing are responsible for most of the world's troubles. It would indeed be novel to maintain that our social and political systems have been molded by the music that people of every age have played and sung, but we do know that the reverse is true; that the music of each period in history is a reflection of the life, the temperament, and the viewpoints of that era.

It is generally recognized that the songs people sing, particularly the so-called popular songs, provide a year-by-year record of the lives of those people. Superficially, these songs and ballads record happenings of importance, the names and deeds of popular heroes, fashions in dress, slang phrases and colloquialisms, sports and games, occupations and professions, means of transportation, almost everything connected with everyday life. Beneath the surface, however, is even more important information; revelation of states of minds and points of view. Such a record is found not only in the words of songs, but in the spirit of the music itself, in its very style and idiom. If we bear in mind the character and surroundings of the people for whom the music of each age was written, we shall understand their music more clearly. Conversely, the student of history will do well to become familiar with the representative music of the age he is studying. It provides a vivid description of the background that produced historical events, and explains why people acted as they did. Honest music, that which is sincere, is invariably an expression of the era that produced it.

Take, for example, the merry lilt of the English madrigals from the sixteenth century. These songs embody the underlying spirit of Merrie England in the days of the first Queen Elizabeth, when Britain was growing rich and enjoying the things that come with economic prosperity. There was joy in life, and people sang and danced to the jolly strains of music by Byrd and Gibbons.

Moving on a century, to Continental Europe, we approach an era when outer forms become more important than inner thoughts. Instead of being the unrestrained voicing of joy or sorrow, emotional expressions are more polished. Tenderness, rather than passion, marks the art of the day, and beauty is fragile and delicate. The placid beauty of Gluck's melodies is characterized by restraint and chaste refinement.

Johann Sebastian Bach lived in an age (1685–1750) when men did not wear their hearts on their coatsleeves. Thus, superficially, Bach seems to be preoccupied with form and structure, and the emotional depths of his works, almost unfathomable, are apparent only to those who are familiar with them. It was undoubtedly the early eighteenth-century insistence on form that lent this aspect to Bach's music.

This was also an age when the princely rulers of Europe

showed their power through costly and elaborate architecture, and we find the composers of the day, Bach included, showing an intense devotion to detail, decorating
their music with delicate instrumental patterns that were
continually repeated and imitated contrapuntally.

In the eighteenth century, concert music was not for the
people, but for the nobility. In the preceding chapter we
found that concerts were mostly given in the palaces of
kings and princes, not in public concert halls. The musician
was not a man of social rank; he generally ate his meals in
the servants' hall. Consequently we find a lowly and humble
spirit whenever a musician addressed his patron. Today
the great Bach has a seat with the immortals, but read the
words he addressed to the Margrave of Brandenburg, who
is known to us only because he commissioned six concertos
from Johann Sebastian Bach. In his letter the composer
begged the Margrave not to judge the imperfections of the
concertos "by the severity of the fine and delicate taste that
every one knows You to have for music, but rather to consider benignly the profound respect and the very humble
obedience to which they are meant to testify."

It was naturally the taste of the princely patrons of music
that determined the style of music written by composers
dependent on these aristocrats for support. And the music,
in turn, gives us an intimate picture of the life at their courts.
It was a day when art, religion, letters, were highly organized
and designed chiefly for the glory of absolute monarchs. The
luxurious court at Versailles was the model for every king,
prince, and courtier of Europe. Manners were polished and
stilted, and conversations were witty and marked by a cyni-
cism that often became malicious. Although the music of
Haydn and Mozart is filled with grace and tenderness, and
exaltation, too, it is nevertheless highly formalized, dealing
with the artificialities rather than the realities of life. The

dance forms these composers used—the minuet, the gavotte
—picture powdered wigs and knee breeches with silver buck-
les, rather than the rollicking, boisterous good times of Beethoven's peasant folk. Even when Haydn used Croatian
folk songs, he polished them so that they would be fit for
the salons of Counts and Barons. If any indication were
needed to show the great genius of these composers, it is
the fact that their music is spontaneous and vital in spite
of the formal restrictions imposed upon it.

It is often said that Beethoven was the link between the
so-called classic and romantic periods of music. It is quite
true that his early style was a definite reflection of his predecessors, particularly of Mozart, while his mature works represent a break with tradition that ushered in the freedom
from convention of the eighteenth-century romanticists. Compare Beethoven's country dances with any of Haydn's min-
uets and you will see how one was writing of peasants and
villagers where the other wrote of kings and princes.

In music Beethoven was a revolutionary; for his time,
almost a radical. He lived in an age of revolutions, when the
elegant, cynical courts of Europe were tottering. In 1783
the American colonists won their fight for freedom, and
less than ten years later the French Revolution cost Louis
the Sixteenth and the beautiful Marie Antoinette their heads
as well as their crowns. The sudden sense of liberation gave
courage to writers and artists who strove for freedom in
expressing their ideas.

Beethoven was a revolutionary in thought, as well as in
his music. He caught the spirit of the French revolt, and
when Napoleon appeared as an ardent champion of freedom,
a leader who would restore order and prosperity to his
people, Beethoven put him on a pedestal and resolved to
write a symphony in his honor. He began the work in 1803,
and by 1804 the first draft was ready. It lay on his desk where

all who came to see him could read the name "Bonaparte" inscribed on the title page. Then came the news that Napoleon had assumed the title of Emperor, and the disillusioned Beethoven changed the dedication. But the symphony remained the *Eroica*, the portrait of a hero, a champion of the people, even though Napoleon had ceased to be that hero.

It was such music that prepared the way for the romantic era, when the actual content of music, what it had to say, became more important than the form in which it said it. Before the romanticists, music had seemed to be principally concerned with the classic forms—the sonata, the rondo, the classic dance forms, and others; it was afraid to let itself go and to abandon itself to its mood. With the nineteenth century, and the revolts of the common people that led eventually to the Central Europe uprisings of 1848, artists, musicians, and writers felt free to indulge their fancies. Just as the political thought of the day insisted upon more freedom for the individual, so did art, literature, and music become a more personal expression of the artist's own view of life, rather than that of his patron.

The old forms in music were by no means abandoned; composers still wrote symphonies in the traditional sonata form, but the forms became more elastic, and were adapted to the individual ideas the composers wished to express. Harmonic combinations became richer and more varied, and musicians had the courage to make a freer use of the dissonances we shall discuss in the next chapter.

A closer relationship developed between music and poetry, and poetic ideas. Robert Schumann gave fanciful, descriptive titles to dozens of his piano pieces, and even when he wrote absolute, nondescriptive, music in traditional forms, it was always the personal expression of his poetic nature. The slow movements—from his symphonies, his Piano Quintet, his Piano Concerto—are far more intense and foreboding than the works that come from an earlier century.

Chopin filled his works with sorrow for the tribulations of his native Poland and he also achieved freedom from many of the restrictions of musical convention. He advanced the development of free forms—the fantasy, the impromptu, the ballade—which are forms determined by the musical material itself.

The lovely melodies of Franz Schubert were aimed directly at the hearts of the people around him; they were not designed for lords and ladies in silks and satins. Schubert reflected the time in which he lived, as well as his own lovable nature.

Like Beethoven, Richard Wagner was a freethinker in his philosophy, as well as in his music. During the Revolutions of 1848 his political ideas became so widely known that he was forced to flee to Zurich and live in exile for nearly twelve years. In some of his music-dramas he embodied his social and political ideas. The *Ring of the Nibelungs* was a protest against forces that Wagner considered evil. And in regard to the music itself, it was the background of the age he lived in that made Wagner dissatisfied with the restrictions that had enslaved the music of an earlier day. He used his great genius to free music from its shackles.

That is the spirit we feel when we listen to the overpowering masterpieces Wagner left us—the upward reaching of a great soul (and he was that in spite of his selfishness and disloyalty to his friends) who longed to be rid of the pettiness of earthly things; a surging that had no patience with formality or even politeness. As we look at history, we realize that this music could not possibly have been composed in the days of Bach, of Haydn, or of Mozart.

The rise of nationalism in music was another movement that had its origin in nineteenth-century history. Just as the coming of democracy dethroned kings and gave to the peoples a new consciousness of their rights and privileges, so also, with the old barriers swept away, and with small duchies overthrown, there came the idea that people speaking the same language and sharing the same customs should be politically united as nations. Thus the political upheavals ushered in not only the romantic era in the arts, but also a feeling for nationalism. Mikhail Glinka, in Russia, was one of the first to express this spirit, and his opera, *A Life for the Tsar*, is generally regarded as the foundation of a distinctively Russian music. Its themes were based largely on Russian folk songs Glinka had heard in his youth, and some of the music was so true to the life of the lower classes of society that a group of noblemen sneeringly called it "the music of coachmen." Following Glinka were other composers of the Russian nationalist school: Borodin, Mussorgsky, Balakirev, Glazunov, Rimsky-Korsakov.

As states became composed of citizens, rather than subjects, the ideas and emotions of nationality were free to develop. The type of thought that shaped institutions and governments also affected the music of those peoples and races that were the most nationalistic in spirit. Czechoslovakia, a nation whose political freedom was denied for several centuries, was typical of this movement. As far back as 1620 the Czechs and Slovaks were brought under the rule of the Austrian Hapsburgs. They were forbidden to speak their own language, and their rulers sought to stamp out all traces of the Czech national spirit. Beneath the surface, however, the national feeling was kept alive, and was probably made more vital by the very oppression that sought to destroy it. In 1859 the restrictions were somewhat relaxed, and Bohemian artists came forward who were filled with the national spirit of their countrymen. The leading composer to express this spirit was Bedřich Smetana, and his opera,

The Bartered Bride, contains many of the songs and dances of his homeland. After Smetana came Antonin Dvořák, whose *Slavonic Dances* vividly express the color and life of his countrymen. ,

Jan Sibelius (1865——) is one of the most nationalistic of composers, and is universally recognized as the musical voice of Finland. As this is written he is still living at the age of 91, and because his works have been among the most performed of those by present-day composers, he is often looked upon as a modern composer. It is true that his music is contemporary in time, but in spirit he is actually a romanticist, heroic and epic, expressing with rare eloquence the aspirations of his fellow-countrymen. His idiom is unmistakably his own, but it does not enter twentieth-century experimental fields. His First Symphony derived almost directly from Tchaikovsky. In the Second Symphony, composed in 1901, he managed to cast aside the reminders of Tchaikovsky, and wrote a work that the Finns accepted as an expression of their revolt against oppression. Its climaxes rise to exultant heights. The earlier tone poem, *Finlandia,* composed in 1899, expressed so fervently the national spirit of the Finns that its performance was at one time forbidden by the Russian government.

Sibelius's seven symphonies, as well as his tone poems and the Violin Concerto, represent a progressive series of steps in the composer's development. He has devised his own structures and evolved his own melodic harmonic style, neither startling nor revolutionary, but altogether typical of Sibelius and of Finland.

In Spain, Italy, Norway, and the British Isles the music of nationalist composers has pictured the temperament of the peoples, their customs and ways of life, their folklore and legends, and the very climates in which they live. The songs and instrumental pieces of Edvard Grieg bring to us the icy blasts of the Northland as vividly as Neapolitan folk songs breathe the warm sunshine of southern Italy.

National consciousness in America awakened slowly. We have been such a cosmopolitan nation, composed of so many races of Europe, that our nationalism cannot take the form of a unified racial expression, but must be a spirit that comes from a welding of all the elements that make up our population. True Americanism in art, music, and literature must be based on our ideals, our aspirations, our institutions, and our philosophy. In the twentieth century, when we have become independent in thought, just as we became independent in action a century before, our national spirit is asserting itself, and our composers are writing music that is not a mere reflection of European music, but that actually springs from the cities, the factories, and the countryside of America.

The American, Edward MacDowell (1861–1908), was closely akin to the Norwegian Grieg in being an intense individualist. Like Grieg he developed a style that was so characteristic of himself that it is easily recognized as almost a trade-mark. Yet while MacDowell was eager to encourage and help to develop a group of composers who would be distinctively American, he did not believe that nationalism in music could be consciously acquired. Returning to America at the time the Bohemian Dvořák was resident in this country and was urging American composers to turn to Negro and Indian folk music as a reservoir of native material, MacDowell disagreed, for he did not think that our music could become typically American merely by borrowing tunes that had originated on our soil. He felt that nationalism is an extraneous element that has no part in pure art. Rather than depend on folk music, the composer to write truly American music must arrive at "the youthful optimistic vitality and the undaunted tenacity that characterizes the American." Therefore, although he was a postromantic in feeling and his music shows a Celtic spirit tempered by German romanticism, he considered that as an American he was writing American music.

Howard Hanson (1896———), director of the Eastman School of Music and one of our leading contemporary composers, has been able in his teaching to pass to his composition pupils his altogether sound ideas on nationalism in American music. Himself of Swedish descent, he has shown his Scandinavian heritage most distinctly in such works as his *Nordic Symphony,* and yet his own characteristically American viewpoint has tempered his heritage so that it is altogether recognizable as belonging to this country.

Hanson believes that every race must write its own music, and that truly American music must come out of the life of America. To him American music is simply music written by Americans, and it does not matter whether the composers are descendants of New England or Virginia settlers, or whether they are the sons or daughters of recently arrived immigrants. He is not an advocate of anything that might be termed an American "school" in music, but he does believe that American music has acquired nationalistic traits, in the definite personalities of many of our younger composers, and in the spiritual individuality of their works.

There has been nationalism in Latin America as well as in the United States. Curiously, one of the most national of the South Americans, the Brazilian Heitor Villa-Lobos (1887———), is at the same time one of the most international of composers. According to Howard Hanson's definition Villa-Lobos would be distinctly a Brazilian composer for he was born in Rio de Janeiro and still makes his home there, yet he has written every conceivable kind of music. By 1956 he had completed over two thousand works.

Doubtless the indigenous music of his native land has played a part in shaping the all-inclusive Villa-Lobos idiom, if anything that is so multisided could be called an idiom. Many of his works bring reminders of jungle evocations and the atmosphere of the tropics. Jay S. Harrison, writing in the New York *Herald Tribune,* has insisted that the "tragedy" of Villa-Lobos "is founded on his own fantastic virtuosity," and no one can deny the composer his command of technical resources in composing for the modern orchestra. But, as Harrison continues, "he speaks with such facility that he rarely considers the nature of his discourse. . . . As a result, his pieces sound for all the world like a tonal equivalent of a patchwork quilt."

In his series of thirteen orchestral pieces entitled *Chôros,* Villa-Lobos attempts what he terms a "personal synthesis" of various types of Brazilian music. The word "Chôros" is the Portuguese for serenade. In another set of orchestral works, *Bachianas Brasileiras,* he has tried to show how Bach might have handled melodic material indigenous to his native country.

We find, then, that all movements and changes—political, social, economic—that have affected the direction and course of human life have shaped the character of the music of various ages, just as they have affected literature and the other arts. After romanticism came postromanticism, somewhat decadent, and often filled with the neuroticism of a Tchaikovsky. This was an era of general decadence, when new changes were on the horizon, but when established customs were still so firmly intrenched that to question them was to place oneself apart from convention. The conventions and the traditions had grown soft, however, and lacked the rugged vitality of an earlier century, when they themselves had been revolutionary, and had replaced those of a still earlier day.

And so we come to our own time, when our music is showing such startling changes, such radical departures from

older music, that it seems to the traditionalist to be nothing
but inexcusable noise. But once again we have merely to
consider the events of our own time to find the reason. Even
before the first World War, life had become more complex
than it had ever been before. The changes that have occurred
so rapidly and so suddenly would have required centuries
in the Middle Ages. Science and invention have made such
rapid strides in the last quarter-century that civilization will
require several generations to catch up with them, and to
learn how to use their products intelligently. Where the first
World War seemed to be a liberation of oppressed peoples—
Czechoslovakia, Poland, Finland—the second World War
was caused by the resubjugation of free peoples by totali-
tarian states. When the Allied victory liberated enslaved
nations from the Fascist yoke another aggressor arose to make
satellites of nations that had temporarily regained their independence. And now the art of these peoples is controlled
by those who govern them; composers may write only such
music as embodies the current ideology of political dictator-
ships.

In America we are free to voice our feelings, and so are
those composers from abroad who have come to our shores.
America has become the cradle of an art that will tell the
future historian how people felt and acted in these troubled
times.

Our modern music tells of the feverish pace at which we
are living. When we dance, we have not the patience for
the slow steps of the minuet, or the smooth, gliding motions
of the waltz; we spend our energies on the feverish rhythms
and motions of the latest dances. Life is so much more complex that our young people are as sophisticated as their
grandfathers, and as wise, if not wiser, in the affairs of the
world. So our music is complex and sophisticated, and much

of it, particularly our popular music, appeals chiefly to the younger generation.

It is, perhaps, the noisiness and confusion of our modern music that disturb us most. But they, too, are a direct reflection of modern life. Carl Engel wrote of this in 1928, in an article entitled "Harking Back and Looking Forward":

"What we need most of all is an explanation for the probable connection between the latest changes in music and the increase in noise. The progress of music is based on and conditioned by the necessity of constantly overcoming fatigue. And the fatigue of the ear has been hastened or aggravated by the alarming increase in noise to which modern life is subjecting us. Probably our whole nervous system is affected by it, and not to its profit. Where two hundred years ago melodious street-calls announced the approach of itinerant vendors and the song of an ungreased axle-tree merely emphasized the ordinary stillness, we have now the involved and strident counterpoint of traffic over an ostinato of policemen's whistles and automobile horns. The timid tinkle of the spinet has been replaced by the aggressive tones of the 'loud speaker.' Loudness and coarseness go hand in hand. Pandemonium in the street, and the home a jazz dive or a roaring Chautauqua—truly the art of music is hard put to devise new stimuli wherewith to counteract the growing aural disturbance. The wonderful and consoling fact is that music, apparently, is equal to any occasion." [1]

It is significant that dissonance in itself does not bother our young people in the least. They have been brought up on it and in the field of "popular" music have not been compelled to make the adaptation from the leisurely synco-

[1] *Musical Quarterly*, January, 1928.

pation of ragtime to the frenetic chaos of modern hot jazz. Perhaps, then, it is because older ears are tuned to the nineteenth century that they are constantly comparing our new music with that of their youth. If they had never heard Beethoven or Mozart, Schoenberg and Stravinsky might not sound strange at all. Certainly traditional Hindu music seems perfectly natural to the Hindus, yet to us its scales are strange and new, and its rhythms almost incomprehensible.

We may well wonder what the music of the future will be, and where some of the recent experiments may take us. There are of course distinct signs of a reaction from some of the more bizarre extremities of the past quarter-century, and we shall find in our later chapters how the younger composers are less concerned with the methods they use than with what they actually have to say. They adopt what they think will serve their purpose from the various devices they have learned and, not fearing sometimes to write even a simple tonic triad, they combine them into a medium for expressing in their own way the emotions that have caused them to write their music.

Whatever course the development of modern music takes, of one thing we may be certain: it will definitely reflect its background, and the ultimate fate of civilization will be vividly recorded in the music that is composed during the coming years. Aspirations, ideals, as well as frustrations, will prove the determining factors in shaping this art expression, and the various devices and patterns of atonality, polytonality, and others that we shall discuss in succeeding chapters, will be only the means by which the composer will convey his inner thoughts to his audience.

3

DISSONANCE—
THE SALT AND PEPPER
OF MUSIC

IF IT WERE NOT FOR DISSONANCE, MUSIC WOULD BE AN ALTO-
gether insipid affair. Listening to it would prove monotonous and cloying, just like reading a novel in which all the
characters are annoyingly good, and everything connected
with the plot is Utopian. The pleasant things of life are
pleasant in contrast to the unpleasant, and it's because bad
things exist that we enjoy the good ones.

Food without salt is unexciting and tasteless, and some
dishes require a liberal sprinkling of pepper to add zest
and tang to their flavor. Even garlic, that noxious cousin
to the onion, has its uses on occasion, and within reason.

The degree of seasoning required to make food interesting
and palatable varies with races and with individuals. Mexican tamales are not to be indulged in lightly or indiscrimi-
nately by those who are not used to them, and the quantities
of garlic necessary to the well-being of Italians would prove
nauseating to an Englishman. Even the taste for such ordinary household ingredients as salt and pepper varies so
much among members of the same family that every dining
table offers salt and pepper shakers so that each person may
season his food according to his liking.

It is the same with the dissonances we hear in our music.
Some of us like them used sparingly, while others, particularly the young people, want them piping hot. The more
dissonances we hear, however, the more accustomed we become to them. Consequently, the development and evolu-

tion of music through the centuries has been marked by an
increasing use of dissonant combinations. Hermann Helmholtz, the German scientist, wrote that no sharp line can be
drawn between consonances and dissonances, aesthetically,
because the boundary that separates them changes as tonal
systems change in the course of evolution. In other words,
the dissonances of yesterday become the consonances of
today.

Thus, the use of the term "dissonance" is elastic. Its most
commonly accepted meaning is that of a harsh-sounding
combination of sounds, but of course the degree of harshness will vary according to the experience and taste of the
listener. The words "consonance" and "dissonance" are derived from the Latin: "consonance" from "consonare"—to
sound together, to agree; and "dissonance" from "dissonare"
—to sound apart, or disagree in sound. The *Encyclopédie de
la musique du conservatoire* defines dissonance as "sounding twice," designating "the effect produced by two sounds
which seem to repulse each other and give to the ear the impression of two distinct sounds, although struck together." [1]

While musically, or aesthetically, a dissonance is a harsh
combination of sounds, in effect it is a chordal combination
that so disturbs the ear that it requires satisfaction and ap-
peasement in the chords that follow. The most elementary
example of this principle is found in the so-called dominant
seventh chord:

If this chord is heard by itself, the musical ear demands something to follow it, something that will answer, or resolve, the unfinished feeling aroused by its dissonance. Thus, the chord is followed by another that pacifies the disturbed musical sense:

The second chord is known as the "resolution" of the first, because it resolves the disturbance the dissonance has caused. When properly resolved, a dissonance is not necessarily unpleasant; it affords contrast to the more comfortable sounds. This brings to mind the man who said that the most wonderful sensation in the world is a good itch—if you can scratch it.

Hearing the first chord alone is like having a man upstairs drop one shoe without the other. A story is told of a music pupil who wanted to revenge himself upon his teacher. After the teacher was in bed, the pupil played the first of the chords on the piano, and hid behind the curtains to see what would happen. In ten or fifteen minutes the teacher groped his way down the stairs, stumbled into the music room and, finding the piano keyboard, struck the second chord. Then, muttering to himself, he went back to bed.

It is in this matter of resolutions that we find a fundamental difference between the music of the old masters and that of modern times. The older composers used dissonances, plenty of them, but they were almost invariably resolved by consonances. Modernists use dissonances alone, and deny the listener's ear the relief of conventional resolutions. Dr. Burney, the eighteenth-century music historian, wrote in

1770 that discord "seems to be as much the essence of music, as shade is in painting." He qualified his observation by stating that *"provided the ear be at length made amends, there are few dissonances too strong for it."*

In the first Prelude of his *Well-Tempered Clavichord*, Bach wrote a chord that would suit the purpose of almost any present-day composer:

He followed it, however, with two chords of resolution that give the ear its satisfaction:

In the following passage from Bizet's *Le Carillon* (from the *L'Arlésienne Suite,* No. 1) the composer used a particularly biting dissonance at the point marked A, which is not fully resolved until the point marked B is reached in the following measure:

etc.

The satisfaction from the eventual resolution is complete, however, even though it was delayed.

Wagner developed a type of dissonance that was severely attacked at first, but which soon became such an accepted part of the musical vocabulary that it is difficult to understand why it was ever considered dissonant. The technical term for this innovation was "chromaticism," or chromatic harmonies. This is an accurate phrase for describing these chords, for they add considerable color to music, and they vastly increased Wagner's powers of emotional expression.

The basis of chromatic harmonies is a constant changing of key in a musical passage; a passing from one key to another, which is known as "modulation." Technically, a chromatic melody or harmonic progression is one that uses tones foreign to the key in which it is written. A melody or harmonic progression that remains in its own key is called a "diatonic" melody, or progression. Thus, a diatonic melody in the key of C major is one that uses no tones except those represented by the white keys on a piano keyboard. If, however, an F sharp is introduced, that is a chromatic tone, and the melody and the accompanying harmony become chromatic, since F sharp does not belong in the key of C.

A striking example of Wagner's chromaticism is found in the opening measures of the Prelude to *Tristan und Isolde*:

Although the key signature of this passage contains no sharps and flats, showing that it is written in the key of A minor, there is only one chord in these first seven measures that properly belongs in that key (the final chord in the third measure). In fact, the key signature of A minor remains un-

changed for the first forty-three measures of the Prelude,
although the music is actually in that key at only a few
places, and then only momentarily.

After Wagner, the composer to cause the greatest furor
and disturbance among music-lovers and critics was Richard
Strauss (1864–1949). In his tone poems Strauss was something of a realist, using descriptive and highly discordant
effects to portray the scandalous adventures and horrible
end of *Till Eulenspiegel,* and to lend dramatic force to
others of his musical narratives. He opened the way to a
flood of dissonance from his followers that at first seemed
terrifying, but has gradually become so assimilated by music
lovers that Strauss no longer seems a modernist. At the
end of *Also sprach Zarathustra* (*Thus Spake Zarathustra*),
another of his tone poems, he introduced an effect that was
highly novel at the time: having the bass instruments sound
a chord in one key, and the upper instruments a chord in
another key, so closely together that the ear actually hears
the two chords at the same time. This was a forerunner of
a device known as "polytonality," which will be discussed in
more detail in a later chapter.

Strauss's early works were written in a classic-romantic
style that derived directly from the Schumann-Brahms school.
These included his *Burleske* for piano and orchestra, a
symphonic fantasy, *Aus Italien,* and a violin sonata. *Aus
Italien* encountered considerable opposition from contemporary musicians; it was considered extremely audacious, particularly for the "vulgarity" of introducing the popular song,
Funiculì, funiculà. Strauss, incidentally, thought it was a folk
song and did not know that Luigi Denza had composed it as
recently as 1880, to celebrate the opening of the funicular
railway on Mount Vesuvius.

The following years, 1887–89, saw the production of the
first of Strauss's orchestral tone poems that marked the be-

ginning of his truly distinctive contributions to music. These
were *Macbeth, Don Juan,* and *Tod und Verklärung.* With
Macbeth, Strauss started his development and expansion of
the Liszt type of programmatic tone poem and brought
greater musical significance to the form. From 1895 to 1898
he produced a tone poem each year, starting with *Till
Eulenspiegel's lustige Streiche (Till Eulenspiegel's Merry
Pranks).* *Till* is undoubtedly Strauss's orchestral masterpiece;
it is not the most elaborate and imposing of the tone poems,
but it has the most freshness and spontaneity.

Each of the other orchestral works from these four years
met severe criticism. *Also sprach Zarathustra* was based on
Nietzsche's book of that name, and it shared the charges
against the original as subversive and anarchistic. *Don
Quixote* was attacked for its attempts at realism—the bleating
of sheep and a wind machine—while *Ein Heldenleben (The
Life of a Hero),* a musical autobiography, was considered
the height of bad taste. Who was Strauss to consider himself
a hero? The shrieking dissonance of the battle scene from
Ein Heldenleben was a peppery dish for the 1890's, while
the "adversaries" episode, in which Strauss expressed musically his opinion of music critics, was considered savage and
vitriolic.

Ein Heldenleben was the last of the tone poems to achieve
true greatness; the *Sinfonia domestica* (1903), autobiograph-
ical in depicting the home and family life of the composer,
was skillful and complex, but it showed a lamentable de-
cline in Strauss's inventiveness. The later *Alpensinfonie*
(1915) is still less important musically. It is elaborate and
grandiose, but lacking in new ideas.

Strauss gained distinction also as a composer of opera, and
it may be that this is the medium in which he earned immortality. His earliest operas, like his first orchestral works,

were derived from the past. There were *Guntram* (1894),
which showed that Strauss at that time was an ardent
Wagnerian, and then *Feuersnot* (1901), which was notable
chiefly for the moral indignation aroused by the plot of its
libretto, written by Ernst von Wolzogen. Then came *Salome,*
and Strauss, whose orchestral works had been completed in
the preceding decade, started a new career as a composer
of operas that were highly controversial when first produced, but of which the best are today standard items in
the world repertory.

In 1905, when *Salome* was produced at Dresden, people
began to assume that Strauss was fond of subjects of a
decadent nature. *Salome* uses a German translation of Oscar
Wilde's French play, and musically it was the first of Strauss's
operatic masterpieces. When it was produced at the Metropolitan in New York in the season of 1906–07, the directors
were so offended by the dance of the seven veils that they
commanded Heinrich Conried, the managing director, to
take it from the repertoire after a single performance. In
1909, the shrewd Oscar Hammerstein produced the opera
at the Manhattan Opera House with Mary Garden in the
leading role. Public curiosity over the lascivious dance was
so great that the huge theater was filled to capacity at doubled
prices.

Strauss's next opera went still further in bloodcurdling
effects. This was *Elektra,* in which Hugo von Hofmannsthal's
libretto gives modern psychological treatment to the ancient
Greek legend of Orestes returning to avenge Agamemnon.
Where Strauss had mixed decadent luxury with horror in
Salome, he now piled horror upon horror against a background of persistent gloom and despair. The music was
utterly shocking to the ears of 1909; it caused a sensation as
the last word in ear-splitting dissonance. It was recognized,

however, that the composer had not indulged in discords
for their own sake, but was rather investing a scabrous theme
with an entirely appropriate musical dress.

Salome and *Elektra* are one-act operas. The next opera,
again to a libretto by Hofmannsthal, was a full-length work
in three acts. *Der Rosenkavalier*, first produced in 1911, is
entirely different in character from its predecessors. The
libretto is considered one of the finest operatic texts that has
ever been written, and the music, while sometimes heavy
and overcomplex, is so glamorous and masterful that *Der
Rosenkavalier* has become a favorite in the repertoire of
opera-houses the world over.

Some rank *Der Rosenkavalier* with Wagner's *Die Meister-
singer* as one of the two greatest of all comic operas. Certainly it is Strauss's masterpiece and one he never matched
with his later works, even though he remained active and
prolific for another quarter-century. There are those who
rate *Ariadne auf Naxos* (1912) as one of his great works and
certainly *Arabella*, first presented in 1933 and given its
American première twenty years later, is altogether charm-
ing. Others include *Intermezzo* (1924), *Die Aegyptische
Helen* (1928), and *Capriccio* (1940–41), but these cannot
compare with the truly great ones.

The public's attitude to Strauss's works provides a complete example of its changing conception of dissonance. His
innovations are commonplaces today, because the sounds
that were harsh to the ears of our forefathers, and to our own
ears a few decades ago, are not as harsh as they seemed at
first. We actually need more seasoning in our music, and
for that reason good old Papa Haydn does not provide an
altogether satisfying musical menu for twentieth-century
ears, particularly if his symphonies and quartets are heard
alone, without more recent works on the same program. They
haven't enough salt and pepper.

Gradually through the centuries, the aural mechanism and the taste of the music-loving public have become used to the new and the strange, for if innovations prove in time to be artistically valid, if they really add to the expressiveness of music, they are ultimately accepted. So each era has accustomed itself to a new set of discords, and people have come actually to demand them. Carl Engel wrote some understanding words on this subject: "Each new tonal device was an innovation in its day," he explained, "designed to communicate to the ear a fresh equivalent of the stimulus necessary to relieve satiety by way of variety. . . . The proportion of discords needed to tauten our nerves depends upon the individual and the generation. . . . In contemporary music we have learned to demand discord not merely for the sake of contrast, but for itself, as an indispensable stimulus." [2]

We must realize, of course, that the harshness of dissonance is tempered by the musical texture that results from the distinctive tone of the instrument, or combinations of instruments, which produce it. Tones of the same pitch will have an entirely different texture when played by a group of string instruments, or by wood winds, from their production by striking the keys of a piano. When we try on the piano an orchestral or chamber music passage and find the combinations of tones biting and metallic, we must remember that the same passage will give an entirely different effect when the tone combinations are blended by the tone color of other instruments. It is for this reason that piano transcriptions of modern orchestral works are rarely satisfactory; the tone color of a percussion instrument is so unlike that of orchestral combinations.

[2] In "Harking Back and Looking Forward," *Musical Quarterly,* January, 1928.

4

ACOUSTICS
AND THE DEVELOPMENT
OF HARMONY

AT THE RISK OF BECOMING TECHNICAL, IT MAY HELP TOWARD
an understanding of modern music to compare the human
conception of musical consonance and dissonance with a
few acoustic principles. The art of music and the practice of
harmony have been developed according to what has pleased
human ears; they have been evolved by musicians, not by
scientists. Nevertheless, as one compares the growth of the
art of music and the extension of its basic principles with
the laws of acoustics, he finds an interesting parallel between
the two. In other words, men have found most pleasing to
their ears the combinations of those tones that bear certain
mathematical relationships of vibrations to one another, even
though they may not have been aware that those relationships existed.

All sound is caused by vibration. What we call a noise is
produced by irregular vibration; a musical tone by a regular
vibration which may be counted and timed. The rate of
vibration determines the pitch; the faster the vibration, the
higher the tone. At standard pitch, the tone of the A above
middle C is produced by a vibration at the rate of 440 im-
pulses a second. The A an octave below vibrates at the rate
of 220 a second, or half as fast; while the A an octave above
has 880 vibrations a second, or twice as many.

A musical tone reaches the ear through the vibration of the
atmosphere, which is set in motion by the vibration of a
string (in the case of stringed instruments and of the vocal
cords of human beings), or by a vibrating column of air

(in the case of wind instruments). Neither the strings nor the columns of air, however, vibrate as a whole throughout the entire duration of the vibration; they break into vibrating segments that produce what are known as "overtones," or subsidiary tones of higher pitch. Sometimes these are called "harmonics" or "upper partials." The ear hears these overtones even though it does not distinguish them and recognizes only the pitch of the principal tone. Overtones lend an instrument or voice its distinctive tone quality. The flute produces the fewest overtones of any intrument, therefore it has the purest tone, but one that is not particularly colorful.

You yourself can conduct an interesting experiment in overtones at the piano keyboard. Press down the key of C an octave below middle C, without sounding the tone. Hold it down while you strike sharply the C *two* octaves below middle C. Be sure not to press the damper pedal. For an instant you will hear the tone you have actually struck, but as it quickly dies away, you will hear the tone from the key you didn't strike, but for which you are raising the damper and allowing the string to vibrate. The sound you hear is caused by the upper C vibrating in so-called sympathetic vibration with the note you struck. The higher C is the first overtone of the lower C. When you struck the lower C, its overtone caused the air to vibrate at a certain rate, and started the string tuned to that pitch to vibrating on its own account.

Now hold down, without sounding the tone, the G below middle C. Strike the low C in the same manner, and you'll hear the tone of G, not as clearly as you heard the upper C, but clearly enough to distinguish it. Then repeat the experiment with the E above middle C, and you'll have the same result, still fainter, but audible.[1]

What you have actually been doing in these experiments is

[1] If you have a grand piano, you can also get an extremely faint tone from B flat.

to follow the series of natural overtones, sometimes known as the Harmonic Series. This is represented in musical notation by the following table:

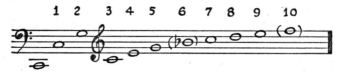

Overtones 6 and 10, enclosed in parentheses, are not perfectly represented by the notes on the staff. Overtone 6 is somewhat lower, or flatter, than B flat, and 10 is about halfway between F and F sharp.

In your experiment, you produced at the start the first overtone of C: the C an octave higher. Next, you produced the second overtone, G. For our experiment we omitted the third overtone, because that was another C. The fourth overtone, which was considerably fainter, was E. With these three overtones, C, G, and E, you have sounded the three tones that produce the common chord of C:

Authorities may differ as to the actual connection between the so-called harmonic series of overtones and the development of tonal combinations in music. It is impossible, however, to ignore the parallel between the two, one a science and the other an art, and to fail to observe that the tones which have been accepted by Western ears as producing agreeable, or consonant, sounds in combination with other

given tones have corresponded roughly with the natural overtones of those given tones. Moreover, the historic order in
which these tones have come into the musical vocabulary
forms an almost identical pattern with the harmonic series.

This brings us to the subject of "intervals," an interval
being the distance between two tones of the musical scale.
Thus, a melodic interval is the distance between two ad-
jacent tones of a melody and a harmonic interval the distance
between two tones of a chord.

For convenience, the piano keyboard may be used for computing intervals. Use the scale of C major, which is represented by the eight white keys starting with middle C, or,
for that matter, with any C, and ending with the C an octave
above. An interval is computed by counting both the lower
and upper tones of the interval, as well as those between.
Thus, the interval from C to the D above it is a second; we
counted two keys, C and D. From C to E is a third, for we
counted three keys, C, D, E. Similarly, from C to F is a
fourth; from C to G a fifth; from C to A a sixth; from C to
B a seventh; and from C to the upper C an eighth, or octave.
Continuing further, from middle C to the D above the next
higher C is a ninth.

These intervals would appear as follows in music notation:

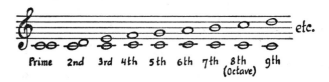

The connection between the vibrating rate of tones and
the Western conception of "consonance" (which may be
defined as a combination of tones that is agreeable and satisfying, as opposed to dissonance) is illustrated by the fact
that the first interval to be accepted as consonant was the

octave. The octave, we have found, is the first overtone in the series, and its rate of vibration is either double or half of that of the basic tone, depending on whether it is higher or lower than the basic tone.

The history of music records attempts at harmony from as early as the ninth century. Earlier than that the Greeks had merely sung an octave above or below the melody when they sang in parts. Harmony, of course, is the simultaneous sounding of two or more tones, producing what we know as a chord. In written or printed music, a chord, or harmonic combination, is shown in a vertical arrangement of notes:

In the earliest attempts at harmony, the only intervals considered consonant were the octave, the fourth, and the fifth. Again consulting the overtones series, we will note that just as the octave is the first natural overtone, the fifth is number 2. In the tempered scale, the fourth is the complement of the fifth, by inversion. In other words, while the interval from C to G is a fifth, if we put the G below the C, instead of above it, we have a fourth, computing downward from C to G:

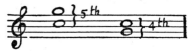

The crude harmony of the ninth century consisted of singing in parts that were an octave, a fourth, or a fifth, from the principal melody. This was known as "organum," which would look something like this in modern notation:

etc.

The chief development of organum was the acceptance of overtone 2 (the fifth and its inversion, the fourth) as forming a consonant or nondissonant harmonic interval with the basic tone.

In short, during these earliest attempts at harmony, the only intervals that were considered consonant were the octave, the fourth, and the fifth.

It is extraordinary that the composers of organum, producing a kind of harmony for the first time in history, accepted the only three intervals based on the first two steps of the Harmonic Series: the octave, the fifth, the inversion of the fifth (the fourth). By ear and instinct they followed a path that science did not discover for centuries.

You will notice that the parts in organum moved in parallel motion to each other; when the melody proceeded upward or downward in the scale, the accompanying parts moved in the same direction. Two or three hundred years after organum was developed, a new style came into vogue. This was known as "descant," in which the voices moved in both parallel and contrary motion, and thus achieved a greater independence:

This eventually led to a horizontal type of part-writing that has become known as "counterpoint." Counterpoint is the combination of two or more melodies in a horizontal pattern, in contrast to harmony in which the tones are arranged in vertical combination. Counterpoint produces harmony, however, for the tones of each component melody produce a vertical combination with whichever tones of the other melodies occur simultaneously. If you can persuade one of your friends to sing Dvořák's *Humoresque* while you sing Foster's *Old Folks at Home* you will produce counterpoint. The two melodies go well together because their succession of tones happens to be so arranged that each makes a consonance with the tone of the other at the principal points at which they fall together.

Counter melodies in orchestrations are a form of counterpoint, as also are obbligati that are played simultaneously with the principal melodies of a composition. In fact, it is counterpoint that enriches and lends interest to the instrumental, or choral, arrangement of any work. In orchestral or band pieces the wood winds, brass instruments, and strings are constantly given decorative passages and added melodies that offer variety as well as richness to the combined effect. One of the most skillful arrangers of musical comedy scores, Robert Russell Bennett, has written an article about scoring for theater orchestra in which he states:

"Taking anything from a whistled melody to a piano sketch from its author to the lighted orchestra pit of a theatrical production demands a great many things besides theatrical training; but if I were asked what the greatest asset one can have in this work is, I should have to answer, 'counterpoint.' . . . The audience, sitting there watching dimpled knees, and listening to tiny voices singing out familiar emotions, has no idea what counterpoint is; but let it be stiff, forced, or badly distributed, and the knees become less dimpled, the tiny voices grow tinier, and the general atmosphere becomes charged with an unmistakable *So what?* What the public doesn't know, which is plenty, it very nearly always feels, and that applies to the good things as well as the bad." [2]

Another form of counterpoint is the so-called "imitative" counterpoint, in which various voices or instrumental parts imitate and echo each other by repeating what the others have sung or played. This is the basis of the contrapuntal music of anthems and choral works, and it is also the fundamental principle of the "canon" and "fugue." A canon is similar to the round, and is constructed on a melody in which the various phrases may be sounded simultaneously with one another. Thus, in the familiar *Three Blind Mice*, the first group starts singing the opening phrase, "Three blind mice, three blind mice." As it starts the second phrase, "See how they run, see how they run," the next group begins the first phrase, "Three blind mice," etc. Then, when the first group comes to the third phrase, "They all ran after the farmer's wife," the second group sings the second phrase, and a third group starts at the beginning. If there are still more singers, as many as six groups may participate, each entering with

[2] *Modern Music,* May–June, 1932.

the opening phrase as the earlier groups come to the successive phrases: "Who cut off their tails with a carving knife"; "You never saw such a sight in your life," and the final, "As three blind mice."

A fugue is a more involved and complicated development of the canon. The term is derived from the Latin *fuga*, meaning a flight, which aptly characterizes the chasing of one part by another, as each echoes and imitates what the other has played or sung. Each instrumental or vocal part in a fugue is equal in importance. The principal theme is first announced by one part, and is then taken up successively by the other parts, as the first part continues to unfold the subsequent progress of the theme. Subsidiary themes, and transpositions to different registers, all treated imitatively, render the construction of a fugue a challenging problem to the composer.

In the hands of the seventeenth and eighteenth century composers, notably Bach and Handel, counterpoint became one of the most flexible and intricate devices of musical composition. The mighty fugues of Bach are monuments of musical ingenuity and inventiveness, so masterful in their construction that accustomed listeners never tire of hearing them.

The oldest known canon, or round, is the thirteenth-century English song, *Sumer is icumen in,* of which the manuscript, now in the British Museum, came from Reading Abbey, and is believed to date from 1240. The song is not only the oldest known canon, it is also the oldest known harmonized music that is frequently performed today, and the earliest existing composition for six parts. One of the most important features of *Sumer is icumen in* is its employment of the harmonic intervals of the third and sixth.

An inversion of any interval that lies within an octave, incidentally, may be computed by subtracting the interval number from 9. Thus the inversion of a fifth is a fourth, of a third, a sixth, a second, a seventh, and vice versa. Therefore the relationship of the third and sixth, the intervals used in *Sumer is icumen in,* is as follows:

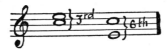

In the early specimens of "descant" the octave and the fifth (or fourth) were still the only intervals that were allowed. With *Sumer is icumen in* a form of descant known as "Fauxbourdon" originated in England, which admitted the interval combinations of the third and sixth. A melody harmonized according to the principles of Fauxbourdon would look like this:

With Fauxbourdon, then, overtone 4 was accepted as a consonant interval. It had required over thirteen hundred years, almost a millennium and a half, for the human ear to become accustomed to the combination of three tones that make the simplest chord in the music of the Western world!

With the acceptance of the third and sixth as consonant intervals, the principle of building chords in thirds came into practice. The common chord, or triad, consists of three tones, of which the upper two are arranged as a series of thirds above the fundamental tone:

In this chord each tone is a third removed from its
neighbor, while the top tone, G, is a fifth from the basic
tone, C.

The next step in harmonic development was the introduction of the tone that corresponds roughly with overtone
6 in the harmonic series, and which is a seventh removed from
the fundamental tone, and also a third above the fifth:

This was indeed a radical departure. Even though the
harmonic interval of the seventh was well established by the
time of Claudio Monteverdi (sixteenth and seventeenth
centuries), it was still considered a dissonance, and its use
was limited by rigid rules and limitations. Most of the pro-
tests that Monteverdi's music provoked were caused by his
free use of seventh chords.

The principle of building chords in thirds was advanced
principally by a French composer, Jean Philippe Rameau
(1683–1764). Rameau also increased the variety of the harmonic vocabulary by discovering that the common chord
may be "inverted" by using another of its tones than the fundamental as the lowest tone of the chord. Thus the common
chord of C has E for its lowest tone in its first inversion:

and G for its lowest tone in its second inversion:

Throughout the entire history of music, the extension of the harmonic vocabulary has consisted largely of adding another third to previously existing chords. In modern music composers make free use of chords of the ninth, and the eleventh, and others with even further added thirds:

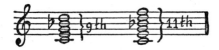

Again, comparison with the table of overtones (p. 42) shows an interesting parallel. In the foregoing example, the ninth and eleventh intervals of the chords (D and F) are next in the series of overtones after the seventh (B flat), omitting, of course, overtones 7 and 9 (C and E), which are repetitions, in higher octaves, of lower overtones. Thus, the acceptance of intervals that had formerly been considered dissonant has continued to have its approximate counterpart in the series of natural harmonics, from early times to the present.

The harmonic intervals of the ninth and the eleventh (and, in modern music, the thirteenth) have not had any easier time in finding acceptance than their predecessors—the fifth, third, and seventh. Although all of them are now in common use, they have, to quote Aaron Copland in *Our New Music*,[3]

[3] New York: Whittlesey House, 1941.

"only gradually fought their way into the musical sun, and each time, a minor revolution had to take place before they were admitted."

While it is neither necessary nor desirable that these pages should present a detailed exposition of the principles of traditional harmony and counterpoint, there are certain matters the reader should have in mind, particularly in comparing modern music with that of earlier times. When we learn that composers have violated or disregarded the rules that limited their predecessors, it will help matters materially if we know what some of those rules were.

The art of harmony deals not only with chords, but, even more important, with the progression of chords; in other words, with the succession of tone combinations and the way in which the several tones of a chord proceed to those of the following chord. These principles of harmonic progression apply also to counterpoint, for while counterpoint is a horizontal combination, or weaving together, of independent melodies, it actually produces harmonic combinations when tones of the separate melodies are heard together.

The pupil studying harmony has traditionally been confronted with a series of "don'ts," rules that he must not violate when he is writing what is called "strict" harmony or counterpoint. The most famous of these rules is that no harmonic progression should contain parallel fifths between any two voices. In short, the composer must *not* write progressions which *were* used in ninth-century organum. The following passage would be "incorrect":

because the progression of G to A in the tenor part forms so-called parallel fifths with the progression of C to D in the bass. The two tones were a fifth apart in the first chord, and each moved upward, in the same direction, to form another fifth in the following chord. To be "correct," the progression should have been written:

This avoids the parallel fifths. Similarly, parallel octaves between two parts were forbidden. These rules were broken on occasion, of course, but unless a composer violated them consciously, to produce an intended effect, he was considered unqualified for his profession.

The use of seventh chords, and of their dissonant intervals, has been governed by well-defined rules, which provide for their resolution and also for their preparation through the chords that precede them. The use of other dissonant tones has also been regulated. Consequently, the traditional rules specify not only what combinations of tones may be used, but what their relationship shall be to the chords that precede and follow them. As the rules have been liberalized and the restrictions have relaxed, further dissonances have been permitted, and composers have been permitted to use them with increasing freedom and independence.

IMPRESSIONISM— DEBUSSY AND HIS FOLLOWERS

To TWENTIETH-CENTURY MUSIC LOVERS, THE WORKS OF CLAUDE Debussy (1862–1918) mark the beginning of modern music. His harmonic devices were so different from those of earlier music that they necessitated the rewriting of many harmony textbooks, while the mood and atmosphere of his music proved so novel that it was baffling to many on first hearing. In addition, Debussy himself was such a freethinker that he delighted in defying convention, and no doubt enjoyed the discomfiture of his teachers. He subscribed to the radical idea that the composer's ear and taste provided a better standard of what is effective than the rules of harmony and counterpoint.

Debussy brought to music a style known as impressionism, a direct outgrowth of impressionistic art and literature. Impressionism deals with the effect of objects, rather than objects themselves. The term was first applied derisively to the work of a group of painters headed by Claude Monet in France. In addition to Monet, the impressionist painters included Manet, Degas, Renoir, Pissarro, Cézanne, and Sisley. As early as 1867 Monet exhibited a painting which he called *Impression: Rising Sun.* Visitors to the gallery who expected to see a realistic image of a sunrise were dumfounded to behold what the artist called "the fugitive changes of nature."

For a photographic representation of what the eye actually sees, impressionistic art substitutes the emotional reaction of the artist to the scene he is painting. It gives a mental image, the sensation aroused by a landscape, a figure, or an object; it is not concerned with reproducing concrete or tangible things. In the same manner the symbolist poets, such writers as Stéphane Mallarmé, use words, not for their meaning, but for their sound, as symbols to suggest moods.

Debussy's doubting nature, his inborn habit of questioning the reason for customs, no matter how respectable, made it inevitable that he should be a revolutionary, and his association with impressionistic artists and writers led him to evolve a similar style in music. He left us a body of works that are marked by shimmering beauty, by vague, filmy, atmospheric effects, hued with delicate tints rather than solid colors.

✓ Impressionism is a reaction against realism, and also against the soaring romanticism of such composers as Richard Wagner. It is, however, directly derived from romanticism, for it deals with sensations and with sentiment. It differs from romanticism in abjuring the grand manner; it has nothing of bombast, and instead of offering heroics, it concerns itself with veiled, mystic half-shadows.

Although impressionism is almost the direct opposite of realism, it was the work of a realist composer, the Russian Modest Mussorgsky (1839–1881), that exercised the greatest influence on Debussy as a freethinker in his music. That was, perhaps, because Mussorgsky represented a complete breaking away from Wagnerism; for while Debussy was an ardent Wagnerite in his youth, he came to feel that French music must rid itself of the German romantic influence if it was to be vital and independent.

Mussorgsky was a musically uncouth, rugged pioneer, concerned primarily with writing music that would be natural and sincere. Inadequately trained, according to conservatory standards, he escaped the German and Italian influences that dominated the late nineteenth-century Russian composers including, of course, Tchaikovsky. Mussorgsky grew primarily from Russian folksongs, rhythmically and melodically. His harmonic treatment of this material came not from textbooks, but from the modal style of the Greek Catholic church. He did not necessarily question the established rules of harmony, for it is doubtful that he knew them intimately; he proceeded on the basis that his own ear and musical instinct would lead him to what was appropriate and effective. This resulted in a harmonic freedom that has set a precedent for the modern composers of a later day.

It is not known exactly when Debussy first became familiar with Mussorgsky's work; probably not when he was himself in Russia as musical tutor in the establishment of Baroness von Meck (1880–82). His first acquaintance with the music of the Russian composer came later, but he was always ready to express his debt to Mussorgsky. They had much in common: a disregard for academic convention, a yearning to be natural and simple, and a high respect for truth in art. Once Debussy remarked that anyone who heard Mussorgsky's opera, *Boris Godounov*, would hear the whole of his own *Pelléas et Mélisande*.

Fundamentally, there was a wide difference in the approach of the two artists to their problems. Mussorgsky had little training, so he could not be said to have broken rules and traditions consciously. He proceeded largely by instinct, and disregarded convention without being aware of its existence. Debussy was trained rigidly at the Paris Conservatoire. He learned the rules and then revolted against their restrictions. Whatever he violated, he did so consciously and intentionally.

His revolt began in his student days at the Conservatoire. To his fellow pupils he complained about the strict rules they were compelled to observe—resolving seventh chords and dissonances; avoidance of parallel fifths and octaves; writing parts in contrary, rather than parallel, motion. He conducted experiments of his own: devising chord combinations that sounded like the bells he had heard in his childhood; adding to his chords the intervals of the ninth and the eleventh; making dissonances that were explained by no other reason than that Debussy liked them that way.

His extraordinary talents won him the Prix de Rome in 1884, but his works departed so radically from accepted custom that they shocked the judges when he sent his music home from Italy. The climax was reached when he refused to write the accustomed overture for the concert devoted annually to the works by the prize winner. The concert of Debussy works was not given.

This crisis occurred in 1890, and from that time Debussy turned from his musical colleagues, and sought the companionship of painters and artists who were following impressionist ideas. His disillusionment regarding Wagner became complete on a second visit to Bayreuth in 1889, and though he still admitted the tremendous power of Wagner's genius, he came to feel that it would stifle those who sought to follow it. He grew more and more consciously French in his viewpoint, and came to refer to himself as "musicien français."

He had already produced his *L'Enfant prodigue*, the cantata that won for him the Prix de Rome in 1884, and *La Damoiselle élue* (1887–88); but his first really challenging works were the String Quartet (1893) and his *Prélude à l'Après-midi d'un faune*, after Mallarmé's poem (1894). In 1900 two of his Nocturnes for Orchestra were first performed —*Nuages* and *Fêtes*, and in the following year the third of them was heard—*Sirènes*. In 1902 he completed and produced the work he had been laboring on for ten years, an opera on Maeterlinck's poem *Pelléas et Mélisande*.

Pelléas is generally acknowledged to be one of the great masterpieces of operatic literature, for it provides one of the most expressive settings of a dramatic text that has ever been composed. The handling of the poem is so skillful that the singers can enunciate the words with almost the naturalness of speech. The orchestral background is at all times an integral part of the drama, neither a mere accompaniment nor yet an independent series of symphonic episodes. Finally, the atmospheric mood of the score, restrained and reticent, gives the opera an elusiveness, a mysterious, shadowy spirituality that makes the pathos and tragedy of the drama poignant and real.

The Maeterlinck drama that Debussy set to such exquisite music tells the story of Mélisande, married to the considerably older Golaud. Inevitably she falls in love with Golaud's younger brother, Pelléas, and finally, in the scene that brings the opera to a climax, the two lovers cast aside their reserve and speak of their love without restraint. The jealous husband watches them, and in a fit of fury kills his brother, Pelléas. In the last act, Mélisande dies after she has given birth to a child.

The tragic story is unfolded, poetically and musically, with a touching tenderness that renders it a moving, delicately wrought love story motivated by authentically human emotions.

In spite of the fact that Debussy made of the drama one of the operatic masterpieces of all time, Maeterlinck was openly hostile to the work. When it was produced at the Paris Opéra-Comique, with Mary Garden as Mélisande, an anonymous pamphlet denouncing the opera was distributed outside the opera house during the dress rehearsal. The authorship of this pamphlet was attributed to Maeterlinck. A few weeks before, the poet had published a letter in the magazine

CLAUDE DEBUSSY

The Bettman Archive

ARNOLD SCHOENBERG

Wide World Photo

BÉLA BARTÓK

Courtesy of ASCAP

CHARLES IVES

Wide World Photo

Le Figaro in which he characterized *Pelléas* as "a work which is now strange and hostile to me," and stated: "I can only wish its immediate and emphatic failure."

It was difficult to understand Maeterlinck's attitude, but the generally accepted explanation was that Mary Garden had been chosen for the leading role, rather than a singer whom Maeterlinck later married, Georgette Leblanc.

After *Pelléas et Mélisande*, Debussy's next major work was the tone poem, *La Mer*, first performed in 1905; and then came the orchestral *Images* (1909–12), which included *Ibéria*. In later years Debussy composed the piano pieces that have become almost as standard in the concert repertoire as those of Chopin: the *Suite Bergamasque* (1890–1905); the *Children's Corner Suite* (1906–08); the *Préludes* (Book I, 1910; Book II, 1910–13); and the book of *Etudes* (1915).

√ Debussy's most revolutionary break with tradition lay in his treatment of the individual chord as an independent unit. The science of harmony is concerned largely with the progression of chords, and its rules govern principally the passage from one chord to another. Debussy looked upon a chord as a color medium which could be entirely independent of anything that came before it or followed it. Thus dissonance became an end in itself, and not merely a temporary disturbance of the ear that must be set at rest by a consonance. When Debussy wrote dissonant chords he had little thought of resolving them, for his chords were entities that he could arrange in any way his taste dictated.

He could never understand why parallel consecutive fifths were forbidden. He liked the sound of them, even in his student days at the Conservatoire, and through his career he used them frequently. *La Sérénade interrompue*, the ninth Prelude of Book I, has an interesting succession of parallel fifths:

Debussy's use of parallel fifths was not always as modern as
it seems; sometimes it reverts to mediaeval practices. A
number of Debussy's progressions are exactly the same as
those of ninth-century organum. In *La Cathédrale engloutie*,
the composer paints a picture of a cathedral submerged in
fathoms of water, and he gains a mystic, stately effect
through the parallel motions of fourths and fifths, identical
with organum:

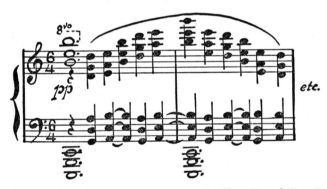

A similar progression is found in another of the Preludes, *La
Fille aux cheveux de lin* (*The Girl with the Flaxen Hair*):

Copyright, 1910, by Durand & Cie. and Elkan-Vogel Co., Inc.

Debussy's use of ninth chords is one of the devices most closely associated with his work. The ninth chord, as we found in the preceding chapter, is formed by adding another tone to the seventh chord, the added tone being a third higher than the seventh (see pages 50–51). The ninth chord is distinguished by its questioning character, and if the chord is unresolved, the ear is left with an unsatisfied problem. The result is a shadowy impression; cryptic, impenetrable.

Ninth chords are characteristic, not only of Debussy's music, but of the works of all impressionists. In *The White Peacock*, a piano piece by an American impressionist, Charles T. Griffes, an unresolved ninth chord suggests the languorous reserve, the detached hauteur of the proud peacock:

Parallel ninth chords give a peculiarly sliding effect, which has been used in recent years by arrangers of popular music. Ravel employed them effectively in his *Pavane pour une infante defunte:*

Another Debussyism is the use of the "whole-tone" scale. The whole-tone scale differs from the traditional diatonic scales by having only six steps, instead of seven, and by progressing from step to step, or tone to tone, in equal intervals throughout its octave length. The diatonic scale, in either the major or minor mode, consists of unequal intervals (see page 34). In the notes forming the scale of C major on the piano keyboard, the intervals between E and F, and between B and C, are smaller than the others in the scale.

These half steps give the diatonic scale a definite shape, and lead to a definite resting place.

The whole-tone scale is formed in this fashion:

Since all the intervals, or spaces between the tones, are equal, there are no smaller intervals to establish a temporary or final resting place in a melody. Melodies built on the whole-tone scale are therefore vague and indefinite, and suggest mistiness and wraith-like shadows.

The most consistent use Debussy made of the whole-tone scale is found in the second Prelude of Book I, *Voiles*. All except six measures of this piece are constructed on a whole-tone pattern. The opening measures start:

Copyright, 1910, by Durand & Cie. and Elkan-Vogel Co., Inc.

√ In addition to devices that may be analyzed according to harmonic principles, Debussy and the other impressionists have added to their chords dissonant tones that cannot be satisfactorily explained by analysis. They are apparently inserted for the reason that the composers liked the sound they produced, or that they were necessary for the descriptive or atmospheric effect. Debussy and his disciples also experimented in what has become known as polytonality, or the use of more than one key at the same time. These experiments were only preliminaries to the polytonal techniques, which are discussed in a later chapter, and they consisted chiefly of sudden modulations, or changes of key, which give the ear the impression of hearing the several keys, or tonalities, simultaneously. Sometimes chords in a key foreign to the passage are inserted, and give a similar effect.

The impressionists also sought freedom and flexibility of rhythm. In Debussy's first Prelude of Book I, *Danseuses de Delphes,* the time signature changes irregularly throughout the piece from $3/4$ to $4/4$. The last Prelude of Book II, *Feux d'artifice,* begins with a time signature of $4/8$. After the first thirty-one measures, the time signature changes with each measure: $2/8$, $4/8$, $3/8$, $4/8$. Then the $4/8$ continues for five measures, and is interrupted by a single measure in $5/8$. In the third movement of his *Sonatine* for piano, Ravel used alternately four different time signatures: $3/4$, $5/4$, $4/4$, and $2/4$.

These are only a few of the basic methods Debussy and his followers have developed, and it must not be assumed that they represent the sum total of the impressionist technique. Nevertheless, the devices Debussy used are so distinctive and so readily recognized that they are perhaps more closely associated with his name than the idiom of any other composer. They have put his disciples at a considerable disadvantage, for when other composers use the whole-tone scale and ninth chords they often seem to be merely imitating their greater model.

A composer who exerted a deep influence on Debussy was a fellow Frenchman, Erik Satie (1866–1925). Satie and Debussy first met when Satie was earning a meager living as a pianist in a Montmartre cabaret. The two musicians struck up a close friendship, and would sit up for long hours after the *café* had closed, discussing their ideas and problems. These conversations did much to clarify Debussy's ideas, and it is said that it was Satie who first suggested to Debussy that he make an opera from *Pelléas et Mélisande*.

In his youth, Satie had little musical training. In 1883 he spent a miserable year at the Paris Conservatoire, but his rebellious nature and his love for sounds that others considered ugly made him leave his teachers before he finished his prescribed studies. He accordingly went his own way, and wrote unorthodox piano pieces to which he gave grotesque and satirical titles: *Cold Pieces; Pointed Arches; Pieces in the Form of a Pear; Unpleasant Glances;* and others equally absurd.

This type of satire gained for Satie a wide reputation as a humorist, although the humor was more often in the titles than in the music. When he was forty years old he decided that he was handicapped by lack of training, and he entered the Schola Cantorum in Paris, where he studied with d'Indy and Roussel for three years. The rigid discipline to which Satie subjected himself did not, however, destroy his individuality.

In a way, Satie was a crusader. He was against anything in music that took itself too seriously; he lampooned anybody or anything that smacked of what we today would call "stuff-shirtedness." Consequently he avoided whatever seemed impressive, and by writing in a naïvely simple manner he caused his detractors to call him trifling and trivial.

Despite the wide reputation he enjoyed in his day, Satie has proved more important for his influence than for his own works, although the latter are in vogue again as this is written (1956). He not only helped Debussy; he was also a factor in the development of other composers, particularly Virgil Thomson and the so-called "Group of Six" who are discussed in a later chapter.

There are many other composers who either had an artistic kinship with Debussy, or proved to be his disciples by becoming impressionists. Paul Dukas (1865–1935), the French composer known principally for his orchestral scherzo *L'Apprenti sorcier*, was, like Debussy, far removed from the realism that was so prevalent during his youth. His work was marked by symbolism, and a typically French delicacy of sentiment. Florent Schmitt, born in 1870 and currently in eclipse outside of France, is perhaps more grandiose than Debussy in his larger works, but in his chamber music he is distinctly an impressionist.

Next to Debussy, Maurice Ravel (1875–1937) has perhaps been the most widely performed of modern French composers. Certainly, his *Bolero*, for orchestra, has achieved a vogue that has had few competitors. In a number of his works Ravel undeniably used methods that have characterized the impressionists; but it is not only as an impressionist that we shall meet Ravel. Unlike Debussy, he remained fundamentally a classicist, even though he adopted modern methods and was something of an experimenter on his own account. Ravel used the whole-tone scale very little, and although he made frequent use of the ninth chord, he was more fond of the chord of the eleventh. Also, as we shall discover in Chapter 7, he was often a polytonalist.

England has produced a number of impressionists. Frederick Delius (1862–1934), like Debussy, was more closely akin to poets and painters than to musicians. A number of his early years were spent in America, on an orange grove in Florida, and he once remarked to his biographer, Eric Fenby, that through sitting and gazing at nature in our subtropics he gradually learned the way in which he would eventually find himself. He evolved a style distinctly his own, aimed not so much at movement and action as at sensuous meditation. Cyril Scott (b. 1879) is distinctly impressionistic in the delicate tints of his harmonic structure; in fact, some of his piano pieces and songs won Debussy's praise. Interest in Scott, however, has waned considerably in recent years.

Others of the English impressionists are Frank Bridge (1879–1941), Gustav Holst (1874–1934), John Ireland (b. 1879), Eugene Goossens (b. 1893), who has been active chiefly as a conductor for many years, and Ralph Vaughan Williams (b. 1872), who is today considered the dean of British composers. Williams showed the influence of French impressionism in his early works. Later he came to be more identified with the movement that aspired to weld folk songs into a truly British idiom. His most popular works are the ubiquitous *Fantasia on a Theme of Thomas Tallis* (1910), the *London Symphony* (No. 2), and the gigantic Sixth Symphony of 1947–48.

Incidentally, Benjamin Britten was a student of both Bridge and Ireland. Born in 1913, he has been a prolific composer since a very early age, having completed an oratorio at nine. Stylistically he defies classification, for he is ever "eclectic but not without savor," as Virgil Thomson once put it. Virtually all of his mature works have been performed in the United States, but none has achieved lasting success excepting certain of his numerous songs, the diverting *Young Person's Guide to the Orchestra* (1945), and the sensitively felt settings of Rimbaud collectively entitled *Les Illuminations* (1939). The latter two are familiar to American ballet-goers as the music for *Fanfare* and *Illuminations*. Britten's many works for the lyric theater include *Paul Bunyan, Albert Herring, The Rape of Lucretia, Peter Grimes, The Turn of the Screw, Billy Budd,* and *Gloriana*.

In Italy the leading impressionist was the late Ottorino Respighi (1879–1936), with his symphonic poems, *Pines of Rome, Fountains of Rome,* and *Roman Festivals*, G. Francesco Malipiero (1882——), and Alfredo Casella (1883–1947). The latter is discussed at more length in the chapter on Neoclassicism. Spain has had Isaac Albéniz (1860–1909), composer of atmospheric piano pieces (the suite *Iberia,* a Tango in D, *Seguidillas,* and others), and Manuel de Falla (1876–1946) whose operas *La Vida Breve* and *El Sombrero de Tres Picos* (*The Three-Cornered Hat*) are widely known through orchestral performances of their dances. Falla was definitely influenced by the modern French school in his orchestral technique.

Poland's leading impressionist was Karol Szymanowski (1882–1937), who was interested in oriental philosophy and mysticism; while Hungary has given us Zoltán Kodály (1882——), famous for his comic opera *Háry János* and for his impressionistic piano music. In his *Epitaphe,* for piano, Kodály uses a modified form of organum.

Alexander Scriabin (1872–1915), the Russian, started his composing career as a romantic follower of Chopin and Liszt, but as he developed, he shared with Debussy the feeling that the accepted harmonic intervals were not enough to express the modern composer's ideas. Consequently, he too made use of the upper intervals of the eleventh, the thirteenth, and some even higher. He also foreshadowed the atonalists, who are discussed in the following chapter, by arbitrarily building chords in fourths, rather than in thirds. Thus, two piano pieces of his Opus 57 are based on a chord consisting of C, F sharp, B, and E. In his orchestral tone poem *Prometheus,* his so-called "mystic" chord is a combination of five fourths, formed by C, F sharp, B flat, E, A, and D.

Scriabin was born in Moscow. He studied at the Moscow Conservatory (piano with Safonov and composition with Taneiev), and aroused the interest of the publisher, Belaiev, who not only issued his works on generous terms, but also sponsored an extended European concert tour in which the programs consisted largely of Scriabin's own compositions. Later, in 1908, Scriabin enjoyed the patronage of Sergei Koussevitzky, who at the time was head of the Russian Music Publishing Society. This organization offered him a substantial yearly retainer, and Koussevitzky engaged him for a tour of the Volga cities with his orchestra.

As a composer, Scriabin passed through definitely marked stages of development. At the start, he was strongly influenced by Chopin, and being an excellent pianist himself, he naturally composed a long list of piano pieces. Some of them have become enormously popular, particularly the etudes and the preludes. About the turn of the century he began to evolve his more advanced style, and the harmonic structure of his works became widely discussed. For a time he ranked with Debussy as a symbol of modernism, particularly when he came under the influence of a theosophy circle in Brussels in 1908–10, and the mystic strain in his music became more pronounced. His major works reflect this influence, and show him seeking an essential relation between art and religion. In *Prometheus* (1909–10) he conceived an affinity, spiritual as well as scientific, between tone and color, and he made provision for prescribed colors to be thrown on a screen while the music was being performed. The work was only once performed in this manner, however; at Carnegie Hall, New York, in 1915. The results were not sufficiently convincing to warrant repetition.

Scriabin's ardent desire to achieve a perfect snythesis of the arts for the service of religion led him to plan a so-called *Mystery* of mammoth proportions. This was never completed, for he died with only the sketches outlined for the introductory movement.

Aside from *Prometheus*, Scriabin's best-known orchestral work is the *Poem of Ecstasy*, composed in 1907–08. This symphony, so called, is intended by the composer to set forth the "Joy of Creative Activity." The two basic motives of the Prologue symbolize the composer's "Striving after the Ideal," and a gradual "Awakening of the Soul." Later themes represent "Human Love" and the "Will to Rise." Concert performances of both *Prometheus* and the *Poem of Ecstasy* are becoming less frequent in these times, although Scriabin's music lends itself so ideally to "hi-fi" treatment that he is reasonably well represented today in the recording catalogues. In some respects it is difficult to understand why they should not be played more often in concert halls, for they are filled with passages of strange loveliness and mystical effects that seem magic. It may be that harmonically Scriabin stuck too closely to the formulas he devised, so that his style became a series of mannerisms rather than a flexible idiom. Certainly, his harmonies were as bold and daring in their day as those of Debussy, but Debussy rarely allowed his chordal innovations to overshadow his musical and poetic message.

Another Russian to show a kinship with the impressionists was Vladimir Rebikov (1866–1920), a native of Siberia, who graduated from the influence of his countryman, Tchaikovsky, and was one of the first composers to use the whole-tone scale. Rebikov has been called the father of Russian modernism. Oddly enough, he has been almost totally forgotten in recent years.

Dozens of composers in the United States have been influenced by French impressionism at one time or another in their careers. The shimmering, sparkling color of the works of Charles Martin Loeffler (1861–1935) make him a close ally of the impressionists. He was profoundly absorbed with Gregorian plain song, and the church modes of the Middle Ages. The haunting, brooding strains of his *Pagan Poem* are like strange incense.

Charles Tomlinson Griffes (1884–1920) was at one stage in his life the most definitely impressionistic composer we have yet produced in this country. Although he was at first definitely under the influence of his German teachers, he came to lean toward the modern French school. In his piano works: the Tone Pictures (*The Lake at Evening; The Vale of Dreams; The Night Winds*) and the *Roman Sketches* (*The White Peacock; Nightfall; The Fountain of the Acqua Paola; Clouds*) he was distinctly a Debussy disciple. His reverence for Ravel exceeded his admiration of Debussy, but he delighted so much in individual chord combinations, dependent on nothing that goes before or follows them, and he had such a predilection for modes and Oriental scales, that his kinship with Debussy was complete.

In his early years, Louis Gruenberg (1884——) was decidedly impressionistic, particularly in the piano pieces, Opus 3—*The Temple of Isis; The Sacrifice; Dance of the Veiled Women; Night; The Flame Dance of Isis.* John Alden Carpenter (1876–1951) used whole-tone progressions, ninth chords, and other impressionist patterns in his early songs and in the orchestral suite, *Adventures in a Perambulator.* It should be noted, however, that when Carpenter first experimented with these devices, he had not heard a single note of Debussy's music. Ernest Bloch (1880——) has had his impressionist moments, too, even though he has gone far beyond the commonly accepted devices by experimenting with quarter tones in his Quintet for Piano and Strings.

Forty years ago to be a modernist was almost inevitably to be an impressionist. Yet, beautiful and delicate as the effects the impressionists gave us have been, they have proved too fragile, too ephemeral, to stand the excessive use to which they were put. The more obvious of them wore themselves out chiefly because they could be adopted so easily; some of them became clichés useful to anyone who could put notes on paper. Even some of Debussy's works have not worn too well. As Aaron Copland has written: "It is his sentimental side that is already wearing thin in many of the lesser works. Despite his musical iconoclasm, Debussy was the hedonistic poet of a thoroughly bourgeois world. There is something cushioned and protected, something velvety-soft and overcomfortable about his music. It reflects a span of life when Europe thought itself most secure, between the years of 1870 and 1914. One wonders what the eventual fate of this music will be in the uncertain world ahead. A time may come when it will seem over-refined, decadent, effeminate. But," Copland is careful to add, "no world that we can foresee would ever wish to do without Debussy's music when he is at his best. At such times he is matchlessly poetic and touching and sensitive." [1]

[1] *Our New Music.* New York: Whittlesey House, 1941.

SCHOENBERG AND ATONALITY

MODERN DEVICES IN MUSIC GENERALLY HAVE BEEN A DEVELOP-
ment and extension of something that has existed before.
Debussy's ninth and eleventh chords were the simpler chords
of earlier composers to which further tones were added at
regular intervals. Wagner's chromaticism was a freer passing
from one key to another. The liberties Schumann and Chopin
took with established forms were merely extensions of the
same forms. Moreover, this evolutionary process has in general followed scientific acoustic principles, even though the
innovations were developed by trial and error rather than
by laboratory methods.

This explains why atonality is the most difficult of all
modern systems for the layman to understand and accept,
for it represents a sharp break with what has gone before
and what has been developed by slow process. It discards
all previous rules and conventions, and starting with the
twelve tones of the scale, sets up an entirely new system.

It is not fair to assume that atonal composers have written
the way they do haphazardly, or that they compose differently merely because they have not had the patience to
master the technique of their craft. To the novice it seems
that the same effect could be gained by taking a brush filled
with ink and spattering it on a fresh page of music paper.
Perhaps the result would be no more difficult to perform or
listen to, but the works of the leading atonalists are produced with as much thought and labor as went into the

works of the older masters. Whatever drawbacks atonal music may possess generally result from an overscientific approach, rather than from any lack of workmanship.

The history of atonality is learned best through the career of its leading exponent, Arnold Schoenberg (1874–1951). A native of Vienna, Schoenberg did not decide to be a professional musician until he was sixteen years of age. He had been a devoted amateur, and had enjoyed playing in chamber music ensembles, sometimes composing violin duets, trios, and quartets for the groups he played with. He showed some of his compositions to a Vienna musician named Alexander von Zemlinsky, a friend of Brahms, and Zemlinsky gave Schoenberg the only instruction he ever had, for he was mostly self-taught.

In 1902 Zemlinsky remarked of his pupil: "He knows more than I do now, and what he does not know, he feels. He has a brilliant and an inquiring mind. And he has the greatest amount of sincerity." [1] Meanwhile Schoenberg had been supporting himself by making orchestrations of other composers' operettas, and acting as *Kapellmeister* for a Vienna café. His own compositions in this period included his famous *Verklärte Nacht (Transfigured Night)*, first composed for string sextet, and later scored for string orchestra; and a symphonic poem for orchestra, *Pelleas und Melisande*. He had also started his *Gurre-Lieder*, for chorus and orchestra, but the necessity of earning a living kept him from completing it until 1911.

In *Verklärte Nacht*, Schoenberg showed himself to be a mixture of postromanticist and impressionist. Having grown up in the midst of the German tradition, he was naturally filled with the intensity of feeling that marked the works of Wagner and the later Bruckner, Mahler, and Strauss. For a

[1] Quoted by Marion Bauer in *Twentieth Century Music*. New York: G. P. Putnam's Sons, 1947.

IGOR STRAVINSKY

Wide World Photo

PAUL HINDEMITH

United Press Photo

AARON COPLAND

Courtesy of ASCAP

GEORGE GERSHWIN

Courtesy of ASCAP

time Schoenberg gave full expression to this emotionalism, and the tonal beauty of his *Transfigured Night* bathes it in a loveliness that is shimmering and starry.

His "inquiring mind," however, was not satisfied. Like Debussy, Schoenberg felt himself enslaved and shackled by his Wagnerian inheritance, and he determined to be a free man artistically, no matter what it cost him. He decided that the only way he could be free was to break entirely with tradition, to evolve something that would be altogether new, a musical speech that would have in it nothing of the past. And what he devised has compelled the listener, as well as the composer, to revise completely his viewpoint toward music and his conception of tonal beauty and effectiveness.

Opposition arose immediately. When Schoenberg's early works in a new idiom were first performed (the Chamber Symphony and the String Quartet in D minor) the hostile demonstration was so violent that Gustav Mahler stepped to the platform and begged the audience to listen to the rest of the concert. Later, when the Second String Quartet was introduced by the Rosé Quartet, the audience again became riotous.

In spite of hostility, Schoenberg continued his course, and finally perfected his atonal system with his Five Piano Pieces, Opus 23. In these his principles are rigidly applied, more consistently than in his earlier piano pieces or in his melodramatic chamber music composition *Pierrot lunaire* (1912).

In addition to composing, Schoenberg was active as a teacher, giving lessons in conventional harmony and counterpoint, as well as gathering together a group of atonal disciples. In 1933 he came to the United States, and made his home in this country until his death.

A literal definition of atonality would be "an absence of the relationship of all the tones and chords to a central keynote." [2] Thus it is the opposite of *tonality*, which, of course, is the principle of key in music, or, to quote Webster: "the character which a composition has by virtue of the relationship of all its tones and chords to the keynote, or tonic." In tonal music, a passage in C major revolves about the tone of C, and the ear finds rest and satisfaction when the tone of C, and the chord that has it for its root, are sounded at the close. Instead of having for its basis the major or minor scale of C, or any other key, atonal music is based on a twelve-tone scale, which represents every chromatic tone within the compass of an octave, in other words, the tones represented by all the black and white keys on the piano keyboard.

This twelve-tone scale differs from the chromatic scale, however, for in tonal music, the chromatic scale is in effect composed of seven scale degrees and five auxiliary tones. In the key of C, the white keys on the piano represent the seven scale degrees, and the black keys the five auxiliary tones. In tonal music each of the twelve degrees is of equal importance. Instead of having one central key-tone, an atonal passage has twelve independent tonal centers, each having a separate relationship to each of the eleven other tones. Thus, a piece may begin on any of the twelve tones, singly or in combination with any of the others, and may end on any tone or chord combination the composer chooses.

The exponents of atonality resent the term. They claim that their music is not lacking in tonality; far from it, it has *twelve* tonal centers instead of only one. It should, they say, be called "twelve-toned," rather than "atonal" music. Some of them call it "pantonal." Nevertheless, the terms "atonality" and "atonal music" have been firmly fixed in the

[2] Article on "Atonality" in *The International Cyclopedia of Music and Musicians*, Oscar Thompson (editor). Copyright © 1939 by Dodd, Mead & Company, Inc.

popular vocabulary. Specialists are by now inured to the indiscriminate use of the terms by nonspecialists.

One of the basic principles of atonal music is condensation of material. In striving to free himself from Wagnerian heroics, Schoenberg felt that there must be no high-flown, long-extended passages in his music. Nor must there be the flowing development sections that composers like Beethoven made an indispensable part of their symphonies. Hence Schoenberg would be laconic, almost monosyllabic in his new music, and he wrote piano pieces a single page in length, some of them containing as few as nine measures each.

He explained this need for brevity in a lecture he delivered in Paris in 1911. "Relinquishment of tonality," he said, "implies a corresponding relinquishment of the structural process founded upon the very principle of tonality; and therefore early examples of works written by means of twelve notes between which no other relationship exists than their relation to one another were necessarily very brief." [3]

Another fundamental principle is the avoidance of consonant combinations, and a rigid insistence on dissonant chords, unrelieved by anything in the way of a simple three-toned triad in thirds, or even a seventh or ninth chord. Thus, atonal music must be written with extreme care to avoid any combinations that would be pleasing to the ear of the man who likes his music sweet. It cannot be composed haphazardly, but requires mathematical and studied exactness to produce an uninterrupted succession of harsh sounds.

In his 1911 lecture Schoenberg discussed this necessity for dissonance: "It is likely that, for a time at least, consonant chords will have to disappear from music if the tonal prin-

[3] Quoted by Marion Bauer in *Twentieth Century Music*. New York: G. P. Putnam's Sons, 1947.

ciple is eliminated—not for physical reasons, but for reasons
of economy. . . . A tonal consonance asserts its claims on
everything that follows it, and regressively on all that came
before. Hence, consonant chords tend to occupy an excessive amount of room, and might disturb the balance proper
to the new scheme—unless some way is found either of satisfying or of suppressing the requirements of such chords."

In other words, pleasant sounds are objectionable because they cannot stand alone as well as dissonances can, so
if atonal composers are going to write short pieces, they must
avoid consonances. One of the methods used to produce dissonances has been the construction of chords in fourths,
rather than in thirds:

This method of chord construction, we have found, was
also used by Scriabin. Schoenberg, however, has proceeded
toward his goal more mathematically and scientifically.

The atonalists also avoid doubling any tone of a chord;
in other words, each tone sounded must be different from
the others—a four-tone chord must have four separate tones;
one of them cannot be the same tone as another either in
unison or in another octave. And better yet, each tone in a
chord must have a dissonant tone to oppose it, a C matched
by a C sharp or C flat; a G by a G sharp or a G flat, etc.

Construction of atonal music follows well-defined patterns. The rules of the system are as strict and rigid as any
of those that limit the student of conventional harmony and

counterpoint. If anything, the atonal rules are stricter. The fundamental basis of an atonal piece is known as the "row," or the succession of tones on which the composition is built. It is not accurate to speak of this row as a melody, or theme, for its succession of tones is subjected to such drastic alterations that it soon becomes unrecognizable to the average listener. The avowed purpose of the row is to establish and reveal the relations between the several tones used. Variations of the series are then employed to increase the number and variety of these relationships.

The first rule is that all the tones of the twelve-tone scale must be sounded before any of them is heard for the second time. This eliminates the possibility of any one tone becoming more important than the others. If C should be sounded twice, the listener might get the idea that the piece is written in the key of C. Once the complete row is announced, the piece continues in a manner similar to the variation form, and the row is subjected to a variety of manipulations and alterations. The intervals between tones may be made narrower or wider (shorter or longer skips and jumps); the intervals may remain the same, but the rhythm changed, elongated or contracted; some tones may be omitted and others added.

Two of the patterns for altering the twelve-tone row have descriptive names: the "mirror" and the "crab." The mirror is what its name implies, an inversion, or turning of the row upside down. When the skip from tone to tone represents an upward interval, the mirrored inversion presents the same interval in the opposite direction, or downward the same number of scale degrees. In the "crab" pattern the row is sung or played as a crab travels, sideways, or, in effect, backward. It starts with the last tone of the row, and then offers the whole series in reverse. The two patterns, the

mirror and the crab, may also be combined, and the row
played backward *and* upside down, simultaneously. Atonal
music might thus be described as music that may be played
forward, backward, right side up, or upside down.

As far as upside down is concerned, much of Bach's music
is so constructed that it is highly effective when inverted
in mirror fashion. An experiment in this direction was once
tried with a player-piano roll of the second Prelude and
Fugue from Volume I of the *Well-Tempered Clavichord*.
The roll was turned so that the holes for the top notes would
be at the bottom, and those for the low notes at the top, on
the spool, and started. The result was delightful. The rhythms, of course, remained the same; but the bass became
the treble and the treble became the bass. Where the familiar
themes leapt upward, the new ones plunged downhill. The
entire work was so horizontally constructed that its outlines
were as well defined in the inversion, and as melodically
interesting, as they were in the accustomed position.

But to return to atonality. It is possible to grasp some idea
of its underlying principles from verbal description, but the
reader who wants to consider them visually and aurally will
be interested in excerpts from one of Schoenberg's pieces.
The following measures are taken from the fifth and last
number of Opus 23, and they show some of the variations
to which the twelve-tone row is subjected. The piece is entitled *Walzer;* an almost ironic title, if you try to waltz to
the music.

There is, of course, no key signature, and the twelve-tone
row is set forth in the opening measure. If you examine it
carefully, you will find that no tone in the upper part is
repeated. Then look at the lower part, and you will find
that it, too, has twelve tones, each of them different from
the others:

In the following measures, the opening motive (the first five tones of the upper part) is changed by having its rhythm rearranged. You will notice, also, that once more all twelve tones are sounded, and none repeated:

In a few measures the five-tone motive takes this form:

and is woven, horizontally, to the same motive arranged upside down and backward:

Schoenberg's Walzer, *Op. 23, No. 5: Copyright, 1923, by Wilhelm Hansen. The excerpts have been printed by kind permission.*

A clear example of the mirror technique is found in a piece by an American composer, Gerald Strang, which is descriptively entitled *Mirrorrorrim*. This is not a strictly atonal work; it is cited merely to show how musical passages may be inverted:

Copyright, 1932, by Gerald Strang. Published by New Music.

The title incidentally is a "palindrome," reading the same backward as forward, and the entire piece in addition to its mirrored inversions may be reversed and played backward from the end to the beginning. The sequence of notes is the same in either direction.

At this point the layman is entitled to ask the pertinent question: how much of this is art, and how much mathematics? Assuming that art has an expressive function, that its reason for being is emotional as well as intellectual, exactly how expressive a medium is atonal music?

It is doubtful that any system that limits itself so strictly and so arbitrarily to prescribed patterns can achieve unlimited expressive powers. Schoenberg himself came to realize this, for he publicly stated that when his system had become fully developed and the music lover's ear had become accustomed to the new tonal relationships, consonances might be reintroduced with safety.

They will have to be included if atonal music is to have the flexibility and variety essential to any true work of art. Expressiveness depends so much on contrast that if the means of gaining contrast are denied the artist he cannot hope to convey his message. In the visual arts there are light and shade as well as colors; in prose and verse there is variety of mood and pace.

In tonal music there are a number of possible contrasts. Rhythmically, a composition may be played slowly or rapidly. Dynamically, it may be performed loudly or softly. Acoustically, the tonal range of voices and instruments affords a variety of pitch from the highest tones to the lowest. The mood color of tonal music may be established, and altered, by the use of major and minor modes, while the sharpest contrasts of all are achieved by the interplay of consonance and dissonance.

Atonal music shares with tonal music only a few of these opportunities for contrast. It may be performed rapidly or slowly, loudly or softly. Its tones may be written in high registers or low. With these possibilities the similarity ends, for atonal music sacrifices the contrasts of major or minor, and of consonance and dissonance.

Aaron Copland ventured a shrewd opinion on the future of atonal music. "Actually," he once wrote, "it is rather difficult to foresee what the future has in store for most music written in the atonal idiom. Already it begins to sound surprisingly dated, hopelessly bound to the period of the twenties when it was first played extensively. No doubt we are badly placed to judge it at present. But admitting our lack of sufficient perspective for judging it fairly, one can even now see certain inherent weaknesses; for whatever reasons, atonal music resembles itself too much. It creates a certain monotony of effect that severely limits its variety of expression. It has been said that the atonal system cannot produce folk songs or lullabies. But more serious is the fact that, being the expression of a highly refined and subtle musical culture, it has very little for a naïve but expanding musical culture such as is characteristic today of the United States (or the Soviet Union). This is not to deny its historical significance or its importance as an advanced outpost in the technicological field of musical experiment. But for a long time to come

it is likely to be of interest principally to specialists and con-
noisseurs rather than to the generality of music lovers." [4]

It is of course true that some highly expressive music has
been created in the atonal pattern. In our chapter on Dissonance we remarked that the discords so revolutionary at
the turn of the century were altogether appropriate to the
terrifying emotions of Richard Strauss's *Elektra*. Similarly,
the granitic, brittle sounds of atonal music seem well suited
to such subjects as those of the two operas of the late Alban
Berg (1885–1935), Schoenberg's favorite pupil and disciple.
The first of these operas, *Wozzeck,* tells of a down-trodden,
psychopathic soldier who stabs his unfaithful mistress and
then commits suicide by drowning. The second, *Lulu,* offers
a conception of womanhood that is expressed by the libret-
tist, Frank Wedekind, in a few lines from the Prologue:

> She was created to instigate harm,
> To lure, to seduce, to poison—
> To murder—without anyone's noticing.

Berg first met his teacher, Schoenberg, in 1904, and in
1913 Schoenberg conducted a concert in Vienna which presented Berg's first orchestral work, *Five Orchestral Songs to
Picture-Postcard Texts by Peter Altenberg.* The performance
caused one of the most notorious concert scandals that even
Vienna had witnessed. The audience rioted so violently that
the program had to be cut short.

The opera *Wozzeck* was completed in 1921 and produced
at the State Opera in Berlin in 1924. Ten years later Berg
finished a tentative version of *Lulu* in which the vocal parts
were completely worked out but the orchestration merely
sketched. Up to the time of his death he worked on the instrumentation, and finished all but the last two thirds of the third

[4] In *Our New Music.* New York: Whittlesey House, 1941.

act. He arranged a set of Five Symphonic Pieces from the score of *Lulu,* which was performed in Berlin on November 30, 1934. Less than a month later he died of blood poisoning, and the scoring of the *Lulu's* last act was never completed by the composer. The first two acts were performed in 1937 at Zurich.

Lulu was not finished because the composer interrupted its composition during the Spring of 1935 to write a violin concerto. This work had been suggested to him by an American violinist, Louis Krasner. Berg was still considering the form the proposed work should take, when late in the Spring of 1935 he was saddened by the death of a young friend, Manon Gropius. Working at feverish haste, he completed in a few months his Violin Concerto in the form of a requiem for the young girl. It proved to be his own requiem as well, for it was not until the April following the composer's death that Krasner played it at the International Society for Contemporary Music Festival at Barcelona (1936).

In 1930 Schoenberg remarked of Berg that he was proud that he had been able "to guide this great talent into the proper channels: towards the superb fulfillment of its individual potentialities, towards the greatest independence. But those qualities of mind and character which were indispensable for all this were innate in him and were in evidence at the very first lesson." [5]

More, perhaps, than any others of the atonalists, Schoenberg included, Berg actually used the atonal technique as a medium for a truly artistic, creative expression. It is true that the emotions and thoughts expressed by his music, particularly in his operas, are morbid and terrifying; but the music is exciting and stimulating, it gives the listener a

[5] Quoted in article on Berg by Willi Reich, in *The International Cyclopedia of Music and Musicians. Op. cit.*

valid emotional experience. In addition, there are moments
that are sensuous and lyrical.

Schoenberg's tribute to Alban Berg contained an acknowl-
edgment to another of his famous pupils, Anton von Webern,
who was also a native of Vienna (1883–1945): "Were not
he [Berg], and our mutual friend and his fellow pupil, Anton
von Webern, the greatest credit to my influence as a teacher,
and were not these two my support in times of greatest
stress; for who could find anything better on this earth than
their loyalty, steadfastness, and love?" [6]

Von Webern's works include compositions for orchestra,
chamber music, and songs. He regarded most literally the
stipulation that atonalism calls for condensation and brevity,
and as a result his pieces are brief to the point of monosyllabic terseness. Works of several movements require only a
few minutes for performance; yet many persons consider his
music sensitive and perceptive.

Those who make a life study of atonalism are often scholars
as well as musicians. Von Webern completed requirements
for a Ph.D. degree at Vienna University, while another
Schoenberg disciple and pupil, Egon Wellesz (Vienna,
1885), won a Ph.D. in 1908, and is a musicologist and music
historian as well as a composer. Wellesz is an authority on
Byzantine music, and the author of a two-volume work on
The New Instrumentation. In addition to writing scholarly
treatises, he is the composer of a long list of works: operas,
ballets, orchestral compositions, and songs.

America has produced several atonalists. Prominent among
them is Adolph Weiss (1891——) who studied with Schoenberg in Vienna. Schoenberg, however, said that Weiss was
too independent a personality to be called his pupil. Weiss
uses the twelve-tone row technique, liberally if not exclu-

[6] *Ibid.*

sively. In his Sonata for Flute and Viola he subjects his row to the mirror and crab alterations, and combines them simultaneously. His Piano Preludes provide excellent study material for the student of strict atonalism. In his *Kammersymphonie* Weiss builds the entire work on two intervals, and his *American Life* is constructed on a single interval.

Wallingford Riegger (Albany, Georgia, 1885) has been an avowed atonalist in such of his works as *A Study in Sonority*, for ten violins or any multiple thereof; *Three Canons for Woodwinds* (1930); *Bacchanale* and *Evocation* (1931), and others more recent. His most important recent work is the Third Symphony of 1948; a strictly written twelve-tone piece, it is nevertheless intensely romantic in conception. Riegger also was a pioneer in writing music for the modern dance, and believes that it is more valid and effective for the composer to write music after the choreography has been designed than it is for the dancer to interpret a previously composed piece of music.

Among the many other composers within or near the perimeter of the atonal orbit might be mentioned Elliott Carter (New York City, 1908), Stepan Wolpe (Germany, 1902), Ben Weber (St. Louis, 1916), Leon Kirchner (Brooklyn, 1919), and Lou Harrison (Portland, Oregon, 1917). But virtually all moderns flirt with the Schoenberg system now and then, including the decidedly nonatonal Aaron Copland, for example, in his Piano Quartet.

7

MUSIC WRITTEN
IN TWO OR MORE KEYS AT ONCE—
POLYTONALITY

POLYTONALITY IS THE OPPOSITE OF ATONALITY. WHILE THE atonalists forego entirely the use of any definite key, the polytonalists write their music in two or more keys at the same time. Most of them, however, content themselves with two at a time.

A number of years ago, when radio was an infant, one of the authors of this book was present at an event that gives a clear idea of what polytonality is, or might be. The Hungarian composer-pianist, Ernst von Dohnányi, was to give a short recital of his own compositions on a local station in Philadelphia. That was before the day of networks, scripts written in advance, and split-second schedules. It was the author's duty to go to Philadelphia with Dohnányi, see to it that he found his way to the studio, and look after him generally.

They had dinner together before the broadcast, and the writer suggested that inasmuch as he might be the announcer, wouldn't it help matters if he told something about the pieces Dohnányi was to play? Accordingly, he took from his pocket an old envelope and jotted down what Dohnányi told him. The first selection would be the Rhapsody in C minor, so he wrote: "Rhapsody, C minor." Next came his *Marche humoresque*. This is a tricky piece built entirely over what is known as a "basso ostinato," or literally in English, an "obstinate bass" that refuses to change through the whole length of the piece. A little four-note figure in the left hand continues its way, constantly repeated and unchanged, from beginning to end.

The author asked Dohnányi what these four notes were, and he replied: "E flat, D, C, B flat." So he wrote on the envelope: "Marche humoresque—E flat, D, C, B flat." When they arrived at the studio, they found that the resident announcer had no intention of letting any outsider do his announcing for him, so the writer hurriedly explained what he had planned to say about the pieces. He gave him the envelope, and told him about the Rhapsody in C minor and the bass figure in the *March humoresque*. He showed him where he had written the names of the notes—E flat, D, C, and B flat, and then went to the piano and played them.

Soon it was time for the recital. The announcer introduced Dohnányi with a rousing pep talk, and, consulting the envelope said: "Mr. Dohnányi's first piece is one he wrote himself; his Rhapsody in—er—" looking at the envelope again, "C minor." At the end of the Rhapsody, the announcer came to the microphone. "Mr. Dohnányi will now play another piece he wrote himself: his *Marche humoresque*, in—er—er," hurriedly looking at the envelope, "E flat, D, C, and B flat."

When the recital was over, Dohnányi wiped his forehead. "Well," he said, "I like to be modern a little; but not so much as to write in *four* keys at once."

Unlike atonality, polytonality is not a system that requires detailed explanation, nor one that has a code of rules to govern its use. It is merely a practice of combining two or more tonalities, or keys, in any manner the composer wishes, and it is used in varying degrees by almost every present-day composer. There is, therefore, no group or cult of polytonalists, although some composers have made more extensive use of polytonal combinations than others.

In certain respects, polytonality is an extension and de-

velopment of traditional devices that go back to the eighteenth century. It may be said to have its origin in a time-
honored device known as "organ point," sometimes called
"pedal point." Organ point consists of the holding or repetition of one tone, generally in the bass, while the other voices,
or instrumental parts, continue their melodic and harmonic
progress, without regard to their relation to the sustained
tone. An organ or pedal point generally begins and ends at
places where it harmonizes satisfactorily with the other parts.
The following example of organ point is taken from the
closing measures of a Bach fugue: No. 2 in the first volume of
the *Well-Tempered Clavichord.*

Bach made extensive use of organ point, generally toward
the close of his compositions, where it would add to the

summing-up effect that establishes the idea of finality. The drone of bagpipes and the sustained tone of the musette are actually organ points.

As music has developed and its resources increased, composers have come to use more than one tone in organ point fashion. Often a whole chord of three or more tones is sustained, or repeated, while the other voices or instruments will sometimes pass into other keys before returning to a chord combination consonant with the multiple organ point. In this way polytonality is momentarily produced.

Still another forerunner of modern polytonality is a device that may be called polyharmony, and is merely the sounding together of two different chords. Beethoven used polyharmony in the *Eroica* Symphony by giving his hearers two tones of a dissonant chord and the tones of its resolution at the same time.

The difference between polyharmony and polytonality is easily understood by realizing that in polyharmony both chords may be spelled, or analyzed, in the same key. In the following combination:

the chord in the bass is the basic chord of C major. Although the upper chord could be considered the basic chord of G major, it is also one of the chords of C major, so that both chords belong to the key of C. Thus they produce polyharmony.

In the next combination, however:

while the chord in the bass is again the fundamental chord
of C major, the chord in the treble (upper part), with its
C sharp, could not possibly be in that key, or in any other
key to which the lower chord might belong. Therefore, no
matter how the chords are analyzed, they are in different keys
and polytonality results when they are sounded together.

In the chapter on dissonance we learned that Richard
Strauss foreshadowed the coming of polytonality in the last
bars of *Also sprach Zarathustra*. In that passage, composed
in 1890, the basses sound the tones of the C major chord, and
in the next measure the upper strings and wood winds play
the B major chord. The two chords are not heard together, it
is true, but the upper chord is sounded while the ear still
retains the impression of the bass chord. Thus, the effect is
distinctly polytonal, as though both were being sounded at
the same time.

We have also learned that the impressionists inserted
chords that are foreign to the underlying key of the passage
in which they occur. Debussy's Prélude, *Canope*, contains
chords in so many different keys that the ear gets the impression of several being played at once, even though each is
sounded separately.

It is sometimes claimed—but incorrectly, as we will show—
that Igor Stravinsky was the first, in 1911, to make significant
use of polytonality in his ballet music for *Petrouchka*. The
so-called *Petrouchka* chord, used throughout the composi-

tion, represents two different keys, F sharp major and C major, sounded simultaneously:

Maurice Ravel explored the possibilities of polytonality with interesting results, yet he could never be accused of adopting any device merely to produce dissonant sounds. He was too much of a creative artist to use any pattern mechanically for its own sake, and when he employed polytonal combinations he did so because they enhanced his truly musical effects. Polytonality intensified the colors on his musical tone palette, and heightened the sensuous glamour of his scores.

As early as 1912, a year after Stravinsky produced *Petrouchka,* Ravel was experimenting with polytonality in his *Valses nobles et sentimentales.* In the opening measures of *Valse* No. 6, the upper wood winds play tones that are definitely in the key of D major. At the same time the upper strings and the horns are playing in B major, while the bass instruments play in C major. Thus we hear three tonalities at the same time: C, B, and D. In *Valse* No. 7, two keys are heard simultaneously: E major and F major.

Polytonality is often considered largely a French product, not because Ravel used it, but because it is so closely identified with the works of Darius Milhaud (1892——), and the so-called Parisian Group of Six, which included, besides Milhaud, five other French composers: Arthur Honegger (1892–1955), Francis Poulenc (1899——), Georges Auric

(1899———), Germaine Tailleferre (1892———), and Louis Durey (1888———).

Les Six came into prominence shortly after the first World War, and became known as "Les Nouveaux Jeunes." For a literary spokesman, the members chose Jean Cocteau, and as musical sponsor, the eccentric Erik Satie. Under the name of "Les Six Français" the group achieved considerable notoriety and became the subject of many discussions and controversies. The six composers led a reaction against the "eloquence" of César Franck, the impressionism of Debussy, and what they termed the "scholasticism" of Vincent d'Indy. They adopted American jazz and imitated the music-hall style. After a few years, however, they lost their impetus and their identity as a group, and only two of them, Milhaud and Honegger, have retained the prominence they enjoyed as members of the radical Les Six.

Milhaud makes consistent use of polytonality. Perhaps this arises from, or at least explains, his kinship with the other members of Les Six, who, in reacting from Debussy's sensuousness, went headlong after brutal dissonance, as well as vivid colors and strong rhythms, turning their backs on anything hinting at sentiment. Milhaud had the conventional training at the Paris Conservatoire, under Gédalge, Widor, and d'Indy, and by the time he joined Les Six he had already composed a large amount of chamber music: four string quartets, two violin and piano sonatas, and a Sonata for Piano, Flute, Oboe, and Clarinet; orchestral music; a ballet; and incidental music to three dramas by Claudel.

The Sonata for Flute, Oboe, Clarinet, and Piano, composed in 1918, is polytonal. In the first movement, the piano, oboe, and clarinet start in F major, and the flute enters with a passage in C major. Later, when the piano shifts to F sharp major, the flute continues in C major.

When Milhaud associated with Les Six, he adopted jazz

as wholeheartedly as any of his colleagues. In 1923 he completed his ballet, *La Création du monde*. This work, based on a scenario by Blaise Cendrars, deals with the creation of the world according to African legends. Jazz rhythms and blue notes permeate the entire score, all in various tonalities superimposed one on the other. Jazz subjects provide the basis for several fugues. It is interesting to observe that *La Création du monde* was produced a year before George Gershwin composed his *Rhapsody in Blue*.

Milhaud's stage works include the ballet *Les Songes;* the operas *Christoph Colomb* and *Le Pauvre Matelot;* and a number of others, including a group of so-called "minute-operas" that last no longer than eight minutes each. His list of orchestral and chamber-music works is likewise extended, and he has four compositions for solo piano and orchestra, and three for violin and orchestra. The Piano Concerto (1934) is distinctly polytonal. In the opening pages the orchestra plays in D major, and the solo piano in E major.

Notwithstanding his love of dissonance, which sometimes becomes downright cacophony, Milhaud is one of the most lyrically expressive of modern composers. His product is decidedly uneven, however, and he has adopted a bewildering variety of styles and idioms. His humor is often crude, particularly when he decides to set a florist's catalog to music for voice and orchestra.

Milhaud's symphonies have enjoyed a certain popularity in America, but among his orchestral works only the rhythmically rowdy ballet *Le Boeuf sur le toit* (1919), *Suite provençale* (1936), and *Suite française* (1942) continue in the repertory. The Louisville Orchestra commissioned *Ouverture Méditerranée* (1953) and *Kentuckiana* (1948), but neither has been recurrent. Pianists sometimes program his *Saudades do Brasil* (1920–21), duo-pianists his jolly *Scaramouche* suite (1937)—both of the foregoing have been orchestrated—and wood wind groups his *Suite d'après Corrette*

(1937) and *Le Cheminée du roi René* (1939). His Sacred
Service (1947) is, with Bloch's *Avodath Hagodesh,* a staple
of the synagogue. Milhaud's lyric Hebraic strain is perhaps
most compelling in such early works as the exquisite First
(1912) of his eight string quartets.

Arthur Honegger became widely known to concert-goers
through two works that achieved a vogue with symphony
orchestras. The first of them, *Pacific 231,* depicts the powerful symmetry and dynamic energy of a great steam locomotive plunging through the night. The other, *Rugby,* deals
with the swift energy and disciplined teamwork of English
football. Honegger was a fellow-pupil of Milhaud at the
Paris Conservatoire, but although Honegger was a prominent member of *Les Six,* he was not altogether in sympathy
with its aims, particularly in its pursuit of jazz. In 1920 he
announced that he did not profess the cult of the music hall
and the street fair; on the contrary, he said, he sought the
cult of chamber and symphonic music in their most serious
and austere aspects.

Two of Honegger's outstanding works are based on biblical
subjects. One of them, *Le Roi David* (1921), is a symphonic
psalm for chorus and orchestra, and the other, *Judith* (1925),
is incidental music to a drama. A third religious work, the
dramatic oratorio *Jeanne d'Arc au Bûcher* (1938), was
briefly in vogue, but principally it has had the effect of
focusing interest anew on the stunning and undeservedly
neglected *Le Roi David.*

Honegger's symphonies have had the special advocacy of
Charles Munch. The Second (1941), for strings and trumpet,
is a grim souvenir of Nazi-occupied Paris. The elegiac Fifth
(1950) is perhaps the most powerful. It is inscribed, *Di-tre-re,*
which does not mean "of three kings" (remembering Monte-
mezzi's opera, *L'Amore dei tre re*) but "of three D's"—"re"
being the French for "D." The three D's are the last notes
of each movement.

One of the most exquisite of Honegger's works is his *Pastorale d'été,* for small orchestra, also available as a piano duet. In certain passages, particularly in the closing measures, this work is definitely polytonal, and in others it uses poly-harmony by sounding simultaneously different chords in the single key of A major. The work is a splendid example of how delicately expressive, and how really beautiful, polytonality may become.

The Hungarian Béla Bartók (1881–1945) used polytonal harmonies nearly fifty years ago. In many ways he was as much a pioneer as Stravinsky or Schoenberg; he experi-mented with involved and intricate rhythms, and at times he departed so far from fixed tonality as to seem almost atonal. His music invariably avoids any semblance of sentimentality and his dissonances are sharp and biting.

It is not possible, however, to classify Bartók as a poly-tonalist or an atonalist, for he was not consistently either. He is more properly remembered as an intense nationalist, and the work he has accomplished in searching out and col-lecting Hungarian folk music, in association with his fellow countryman, Zoltán Kodály, has been of inestimable value in preserving excellent folk melodies. These have shown the world what Hungarian music really is. Bartók used this material in his own works, in highly modern fashion.

In the decade after his death the music of Bartók was heard with amazing frequency. At least three or four of his orchestral works would seem to have been received into the permanent repertory: Music for Strings, Percussion, and Celesta (1936), the stunning Concerto for Orchestra (1943), the Sonata for Two Pianos and Percussion (1937), and the quite accessible Divertimento for String Orchestra (1939).

Bartók was himself a pianist, and a number of his many solo works for this instrument bid fair for ensconcement in the recital literature, although the three piano concertos are not frequently heard. The six string quartets (1908–39)

have proved particularly enduring, as have the Sonata for
Violin Unaccompanied (1944) and the lone Violin Concerto
(1938)—both enormously difficult works.

Like so many other masters, Bartók never had the fame
in life that came to him in death. His twilight years were not,
however, without their belated rewards. Twice in November
of 1944 he stood on the stage of Carnegie Hall and
acknowledged wave upon wave of applause—once for the
Unaccompanied Violin Sonata and again for the Concerto
for Orchestra. A week later he could read of the latter's
tumultuous reception in Boston.

As early as 1941, Columbia University had retained Bartók
as a Research Fellow, and moneys were found (from private
sources) to renew this appointment later. In 1943, after he
had been stricken during a series of lectures at Harvard, the
American Society of Composers, Authors, and Publishers took
upon itself the assuming of all the composer's outstanding
and subsequent medical bills—this for a man who was not
even a member of the organization.

The American composer, Charles Ives (1874–1954), made
liberal use of polytonality, and in his setting of the Sixty-
Seventh Psalm, for eight-part chorus of mixed voices, he
afforded a simple and clear example of writing in two keys at
once. The treble voices (sopranos and altos) sing in C major,
and the men's voices (tenors and basses) in G minor. In the
score, each group has its own key signature:

Copyright, 1939, by Arrow Music Press, Inc.

Ives was a truly rugged pioneer, and became a unique figure among American composers. For years he was known to only a few musicians, and was regarded seriously by still fewer of them. In 1939 his Second Sonata for Piano, *Concord, Mass., 1840–60,* which had been printed privately twenty years earlier, was played for the first time in New York's Town Hall by John Kirkpatrick. Lawrence Gilman, writing in the *Herald Tribune,* proclaimed it "great music . . . indeed, the greatest music composed by an American, and the most deeply and essentially American in impulse and implication." Those were strong words, and while there were many who could not agree with Gilman, the pronouncement focused attention on Ives and brought him belated recognition at the age of sixty-four.

The remarkable feature of Ives's career is that he was experimenting when other modernists were still writing in more or less conventional styles. He arrived at his own conclusions absolutely uninfluenced—note that his *Over the Pavements* was cast in the omnibus tonality of C–F sharp fully five years before *Petrouchka!*

Born in Danbury, Connecticut, he was the son of George E. Ives, who had been a bandmaster in Grant's army. The father was an adventurous spirit musically; he studied acoustics and experimented with quarter tones. Charles Ives, the son, spent four years at Yale, where the conventional music training he received from Horatio Parker did not smother his pioneering spirit.

Instead of devoting all his time to music, he entered the insurance business in 1898, and later formed his own firm, in which he was active until 1930. Composing was kept as his pleasure and his hobby, and because he did not have to depend on it for his living he was able to write exactly as he pleased, without thought of money or fame. It may have been the musical impressions of his youth that shaped Ives's extraordinary music: the effect of two bands at opposite ends of the village green, each playing a different piece; reed organs out of tune; the music of country fiddlers; soldiers and bands marching, some out of step and trying to get in pace with their fellows.

In addition to publishing the *Concord Sonata* at his own expense in 1919, Ives issued in 1922 a volume of one hundred and fourteen songs, some of them simple and conventional, and some in the most advanced idiom imaginable. Recently a number of these songs have been reprinted in commerical editions. The composer wrote for all media: orchestral works, chamber music, choral works, piano music, and songs.

Far and away his most popular orchestral work is the Third Symphony (1904), which won a Pulitzer Prize after its première—in 1946, fully forty years after it was written. George Balanchine's choreographic study *Ivesiana* (1954) has brought needed familiarity to certain of the composer's shorter works. Balanchine has thrice changed the musical requirements to conform with changes in the ballet; in its latest and probably its final form the score assembles *Central Park in the Dark, Barn Dance* (from *Washington's Birthday*), *The Unanswered Question, Over the Pavements, In the Inn,* and *In the Night.*

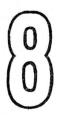 BACK TO BACH—NEOCLASSICISM

AN EDITORIAL WRITER FOR *Musical America* ONCE REMARKED: "We are now, it seems, in the 'neo' period of musical composition. The first thing for the aspiring composer to do today is to decide which 'neo' lodge he is going to join, and thereupon his cloth is cut for him and he wears the robes of his fellows. . . . If he wishes, the composer can be a 'neo-romantic,' or a 'neo-impressionist,' or a 'neo-classicist' or, I suppose, even a 'neo-neoist,' if he is a right smart fellow." [1]

According to the dictionary, the prefix "neo" indicates that the institution or style it qualifies is "new, recent, late, especially a new and different form of a style or school," but the late Olin Downes, writing in *The New York Times*, wondered if "pseudo" would not be more accurate. He asked whether "the exponents of 'neo-classicism' don't really mean 'pseudo-classicism,' or just plain fake classicism, or the superficial imitation, in most unfortunate style, of the shell instead of the substance of the works of past masters."

If all the so-called neoclassic composers were mere imitators, Mr. Downes's indictment would be just, but a vast body of the important music from the twentieth century falls in the neoclassic category, and many of the leading composers of today belong in its camp. As a movement, neoclassicism is one of the significant manifestations of modern music.

[1] "Mephisto's Musings," *Musical America*, February 25, 1942.

The term means a *new* classicism, and it actually represents a turning back to the eighteenth century. Fundamentally, it is the twentieth century turning its back on the nineteenth century; the practical, machine age revolting against the *laissez faire* of the 1800's. The impulse of neoclassicism is the same as that which produced atonality, a reaction against romanticism and impressionism.

Unlike atonality, neoclassicism is not a tonal system. It makes use of any and all the systems its composers choose. A neoclassic composition may be polytonal or atonal, it may make use of the dissonances of Debussy or Ravel, or it may be somewhat conventional. Neoclassicism is a matter of form and spirit, rather than one requiring fixed patterns of tonal combinations. Hence, we do not speak of neoclassic chords or harmonies as we speak of atonal or polytonal passages.

We have already learned how the nineteenth-century romanticists, in reacting from the formalism of the classic composers, became concerned more with the emotional content of their music than with its outer form. The neoclassic composers have reversed the process; now that romanticism has had its day, they, in turn, seem more concerned with perfection of form than with the content or poetic significance of their music. Thus we find the Russian Prokofiev composing a *Classical Symphony*, others writing Concerti Grossi, all in eighteenth-century forms. The difference between the twentieth- and eighteenth-century works is that modern composers, although they are writing in old forms, are allowing themselves the dissonant technique of the present day, and the privilege of disregarding the traditional rules of strict harmony and counterpoint.

Marion Bauer, in her article on "Neo-Classicism" in the *International Cyclopedia of Music and Musicians*, described the neoclassic composers as "more impersonal, intellectual and abstract than personal, emotional, and programatic. The Twentieth Century," she wrote, "in its fear of being regarded as over-sentimental and romantic, sought complete emancipation from the graphic, the literary, the philosophical, and the emotional in music." [2]

We find, then, that the neoclassic composers aim at simplification of their music. Like the atonalists, they eliminate what they consider nonessential, and they condense their material as much as possible. Many neoclassic works are composed for small ensembles, and reacting from the enormous, complex orchestrations of Berlioz, Wagner, and Richard Strauss, they are often scored for chamber orchestra.

It is not altogether accurate to say that neoclassicism is an immediate reaction against romanticism, that the cycle has been a simple three-part pattern of classicism, romanticism, neoclassicism. Several intermediary steps intervened between romanticism and neoclassicism, and the most important of them is sometimes called primitivism, or what might be termed a downright barbarism in music. This represented a reversion almost to the cave man, and involved primitive rites and a tonal fury that blasted the ears of concert-goers. Primitivism undoubtedly had its background in the political, social, and economic upheavals of the first two decades of the century, the years when unrest was first appearing, and when the first World War was disrupting Europe's complacency.

The passing from primitivism to neoclassicism is best understood through the career of Igor Stravinsky, the Russian-born composer who has been a leader in the back-to-the-classics movement. Some critics accuse Stravinsky of an inconsistent adoption of so many different styles that he has become a musical hybrid; but whatever anyone may think of his later works, his career represents a definite series of

[2] Oscar Thompson (editor). Copyright © 1939 by Dodd, Mead & Company, Inc.

developments that are characteristic of the course modern music has taken in the last quarter-century.

Stravinsky was born in Oranienbaum, Russia, June 17, 1882. His father was a bass singer at the Imperial Opera, and although Igor was not a child prodigy, he was reared in a musical atmosphere, and as a youth tried his hand at composing. When he was nineteen, he met Rimsky-Korsakov, who suggested that he study with one of his own pupils. Then, when Stravinsky was sufficiently prepared, Rimsky-Korsakov accepted him as a private pupil, in 1907.

Stravinsky's early works were thoroughly academic and conventional. His First Symphony, composed in 1905–07, is Brahmsian in style, and shows no contemporary influences. A suite of songs for mezzo-soprano and orchestra, however, contains elements of impressionism. These were composed in 1908 when Stravinsky had commenced his studies with Rimsky-Korsakov. In the same year he composed a symphonic poem, *Fireworks,* to celebrate the marriage of Rimsky-Korsakov's daughter. Four days after the ceremony, Rimsky-Korsakov died, and Stravinsky composed a memorial, *Chant funèbre.*

Stravinsky was inactive for a short period after Rimsky's death, but a new stimulus appeared in the person of Sergei Diaghilev, who was organizing his *Ballet Russe* in Paris. It was Diaghilev, and the Russian ballet, who were directly responsible for Stravinsky's most important works. Early in 1909 Stravinsky's *Fantastic Scherzo* was performed in St. Petersburg, and Diaghilev was impressed with the way in which Stravinsky wrote for orchestra. He commissioned Stravinsky to orchestrate two Chopin pieces, a Nocturne and a Valse, for use in the ballet, *Les Sylphides.* Stravinsky laid aside an opera he had started, *Le Rossignol,* and made the orchestration for Diaghilev. Then he returned to his work on the opera.

He had no more than finished the first act when Diaghilev called on him once more, this time with a commission for an original work: a ballet based on a Russian fairy tale, *The Fire Bird*. Stravinsky went to work immediately and completed the score in May of 1910, for production in Paris the following month.

With the *Fire Bird* music a new Stravinsky appeared, a true disciple of Rimsky-Korsakov and an exponent of the Russian national school. The orchestra he used was the orchestra of *Scheherazade*, and the oriental elements of Rimsky's style were amplified and brought up to date in brilliant fashion. It was not Rimsky-Korsakov, nor his shade, however, who composed the *Fire Bird;* in spite of the influences it showed, the music belonged distinctively to Stravinsky, and the *Fire Bird* was an acknowledged masterpiece.

Diaghilev showed his pleasure by commissioning another ballet the following year. This was *Petrouchka*, which was first produced at Paris in June, 1911. This music originated with an instrumental *Konzertstück* that Stravinsky had sketched for piano and orchestra. As the score developed, the piano and the orchestra were given a dialogue, each answering and imitating the other, which brought to the composer's imagination the vision of a mischievous, aggravating puppet, the counterpart of *Petrouchka*, who was the hero of an ancient Russian marionette show, a Muscovite *Punch and Judy*.

As a ballet, *Petrouchka* was immediately successful, but its musical significance was far greater than people realized at first. The music marked a transition in Stravinsky's style, from the fantasy of the *Fire Bird* to realism. The *Fire Bird* had a generous share of sustained, flowing melody, even though it was far more advanced harmonically than the works of Stravinsky's teacher, Rimsky-Korsakov. *Petrouchka* is episodic, loosely constructed, and highly dissonant. If the *Fire Bird* represents the bridge between the nineteenth and twentieth centuries, *Petrouchka* is pure twentieth; at least, early twentieth century.

Most important of all, however, was his introduction of polytonality—"his" for all practical purposes, at least; Ives's *Over the Pavements* was destined for decades of obscurity. It may have been an accident; Stravinsky may have been amused by playing on the white keys with his right hand and on the black keys with his left, but at any rate the vogue of polytonality dates from the appearance of the *Petrouchka* chord (see pages 93–94).

The realism of *Petrouchka* led to the primitivism of the next ballet Stravinsky composed for Diaghilev, *Le Sacre du printemps,* the famous *Rite of Spring.* When this work was produced in Paris, May 29, 1913, it aroused such fury that the audience rioted. The music was so dissonant, so bewildering, that the world was faced "with the alternative either to reject this music as a freakish exhibition of an unbalanced young man, or accept it as a revolutionary innovation." [3]

It is important to consider *Le Sacre* carefully for the moment, for it represents a point in Stravinsky's career soon to be followed by a turn in the opposite direction, from the height of complexity to the utmost simplicity. *Le Sacre* is scored for an orchestra of tremendous size, and it employs crashing chords that were almost unbelievable to the ears of pre-War concert-goers. Anyone who knew Stravinsky's background, however, and was familiar with the *Fire Bird* and *Petrouchka,* was aware that *Le Sacre* could not be a haphazard product, but that its composer was fully conscious

[3] Nicolas Slonimsky in his article on Stravinsky in *The International Cyclopedia of Music and Musicians. Op. cit.*

of what he was doing, and was accomplishing his purpose with a masterful, though grim and almost diabolical, grasp of his medium and his materials.

Le Sacre du printemps deals with the sacrificial customs of primitive peoples, barbaric, brutal pagan rites, and it is not to be expected that such a composer as Stravinsky would have depicted primitive man with the cloying sweetness of conventional harmonies. Stravinsky claims that he would have written this sort of music even if he had not been writing it for the ballet. He says that he conceived it first as absolute music, entirely apart from any plot, and that its rough, uncouth themes themselves suggested to his mind the earth worship of primitive man. Thus, the idea for the ballet came from the music; not the music from the plot of the ballet.

This statement is important in showing that Stravinsky's primitivism was a definite stage in his musical development. First had come the fantasy of the *Fire Bird*, the opulence of the Russian-Oriental school; then, the hard realism of *Petrouchka*; and, third, the barbaric primitivism of *Le Sacre*. The world might well wonder what the next step would be, but it was not for another ten years that it found out, and by that time a colossal war had shaken the world.

Just before the war, Stravinsky passed through a period during which he was absorbed in Russian folklore; and, again using the utmost in performing resources, he composed *Les Noces*, a grandiose work for solo voices, chorus, four pianos, and seventeen percussion instruments. The composition of the "choreographic Russian scenes" which comprised *Les Noces* took altogether seven years, for the war interrupted its composition. *Les Noces* has something of the primitive quality of *Le Sacre*, but its primal urge is apparent through the roistering of peasants, rather than through the barbaric earth-worship of prehistoric man.

While *Les Noces* was as yet unfinished, Stravinsky, still absorbed in Russian folklore, set to music a Russian tale about a deserting soldier and the devil. This *Histoire du soldat*, unlike *Le Sacre* or *Les Noces*, is most economical in its use of theatrical and musical resources. It is theater music that requires only a few actors, and a small ensemble of seven instruments.

Following the idea of writing for limited combinations, Stravinsky continued to write for small groups, even when he became interested in American jazz, and composed his *Ragtime* for eleven instruments. He wrote a little suite of pieces for clarinet, without accompaniment, and in 1919 made a re-orchestration of the *Fire Bird* music, more restrained and less colorful than the original, and scored for a smaller orchestra.

All these intermediary ventures were a preliminary to the actual turning point, which came when Stravinsky composed his *Pulcinella* ballet, produced in Paris, May 15, 1920. This work was based entirely on the music of the early eighteenth-century composer, Pergolesi, and although Stravinsky was by no means a mere arranger in adapting this music, he retained the exact spirit of Pergolesi's style, and kept his own score chastely simple. There was no attempt at modernization.

Pulcinella marked the beginning of Stravinsky's neoclassic period. By adhering to the classicism of Pergolesi's eighteenth-century style, Stravinsky had so imbued himself with its spirit that he was ready to adapt it to original compositions of his own invention. Thus he has completed in his own creative career a cycle that passed from late romanticism, through realism and primitivism, to a pure objectivism marked by a detached viewpoint and a formalism that reverts to Bach and Handel. Stravinsky finished the movement that the Russian nationalists began fifty years before him, in the eighteen seventies. They wanted to rid music of the strangle-

hold of German romanticism, and Stravinsky finished the
job completely and effectively.

In 1923 Stravinsky offered his first original work in the
pure neoclassic manner, his Octet for Wind Instruments. In
writing it he imposed upon himself the limitations that surrounded the early masters. He kept to the forms and the patterns of the classicists, and even though he modernized his
structure by using present-day devices, polytonality and dissonance, he modified the radical elements that had marked
his earlier works.

Other Stravinsky works in the neoclassic manner are the
Symphony of Psalms (1930) for chorus, an opera-oratorio,
Oedipus Rex (1927), and the ballet, *Apollon Musagètes*
(1927). Another ballet, *Le Baiser de la fée* (1928), is based
on Tchaikovsky themes, and *Card Party* (1936), a ballet in
"three deals," describes a game of poker. Since taking up his
residence in America, Stravinsky has completed notably his
Symphony in C (1940), Symphony in Three Movements
(1945), and an opera, *The Rake's Progress* (1951).

Like atonality, neoclassicism places a premium on condensation, but only as a step toward simplification. Stravinsky once explained the need for brevity by pointing out
the essential differences between eighteenth- and twentieth-
century classicism. "For a Mozart," he wrote, "the invention
of the theme, or of themes, represented . . . the maximum
effort; all the rest was made up in great part of a certain
formalism, or at least technical skill had the upper hand over
creative fantasy. . . . With the developments of the theme,
the repetitions, refrains, and necessary 'cadenze,' the half-
hour was soon reached.

"But now that in a scholastic sense this development of
the theme no longer exists, and still less repetitions, . . .
proportions have changed, and a concerto of fifteen minutes

is already a monumental work. Naturally it would be easy
to lengthen the duration, but what would be added would
be nothing but padding, inert matter, sound, but not music." [4]

In reverting to the patterns of the eighteenth century, as
well as to its ideals and spirit, the neoclassicists naturally
turn to the contrapuntal style of Bach and Handel; to horizontal weaving of parts and voices, and the forms of the canon
and fugue. Where, however, the eighteenth-century masters
limited themselves largely to consonant counterpoint, the
modern classicists allow themselves far more latitude. They
are not required to shape the themes of their canons and
fugues so that each part, or voice, will "make harmony" with
the others. Thus the characteristic counterpoint of the twentieth century is dissonant counterpoint; the structures of fugues
are identical with those of a couple of centuries ago, but
their acrid dissonances and biting combinations of tones
belong to our time.

The *Classical Symphony* of Serge Prokofiev is an outstanding product of the neoclassic movement, and is significant in
being the work of a composer who started his career as a
musical radical. Prokofiev was a Russian, born nine years
later than Stravinsky (1891–1953). Like Stravinsky, Prokofiev
studied for a time with Rimsky-Korsakov. His early works
were highly original, and were marked by aggressive
rhythms and bold harmonies. They had a driving, dynamic
power that was all the more pronounced when tinged with
Prokofiev's love for the grotesque. They used almost every
modern device except atonality, which appears in only one
Prokofiev work, the cantata, *Seven, They Are Seven*. The
Classical Symphony was composed in 1917, antedating Stravinsky's neoclassic Octet by six years, and the *Pulcinella*

[4] As quoted by Lawrence Gilman in Program Notes for the Philadelphia
Orchestra Concerts, January 5, 1932.

suite by one year. Prokofiev, then, was a neoclassicist before
Stravinsky, but in his later works he did not follow the movement as closely as Stravinsky has.

The *Classical Symphony* is concise, and written in four
short movements according to the eighteenth-century pattern, substituting a gavotte for the customary minuet as the
dance movement. Prokofiev explained that his idea in writing
the symphony was "to catch the spirit of Mozart, and to put
down that which, if he were living now, Mozart might put
into his scores." Hence, the music is marked by melodies
which Mozart might conceivably have written, but colored
with harmonic modernisms and sophistications that would
have been puzzling to Mozart in his own time but might have
pleased him, however, if he had been living in 1917.

After the war the ways of Stravinsky and Prokofiev became
widely separated, principally because Stravinsky had no sympathy with the Russian Revolution and the Soviet, while
Prokofiev subsequently returned to Russia and lent his
talents to the Communist cause. In 1937 he wrote a grandiose
cantata, for the twentieth anniversary of the October Revolution, to a text made from the speeches of Lenin, Stalin,
and Marx.

Following the production of his opera, *The Love for Three
Oranges* (in Chicago, 1921), Prokofiev followed Stravinsky's
example by writing ballets for Diaghilev. The first, *Buffoon,*
was produced in Paris in 1921. Then came *Le Pas d'acier*
(*The Age of Steel*) in 1927, and *L'Enfant prodigue* in 1929.
Prokofiev spent the last twelve years of his life working on
an opera based on Tolstoi's *War and Peace.* It was produced
first at Leningrad in 1946, and then in a revised and shortened
version in the same city seven years later. America heard it
in 1957 when it was produced on television by the NBC-TV
Opera Company. Critical opinion differed as to whether
Prokofiev had produced an integrated music-drama or a

series of episodes from Tolstoi's novel, but all were agreed that several of its scenes were so intensely moving that they rank with the finest moments in modern opera.

Prokofiev composed also a number of purely instrumental works: five piano concertos, two violin concertos, two 'cello concertos, and seven symphonies, of which the *Classical Symphony* was the first.

Whatever it may indicate, the Soviet period of Prokofiev's works brought a lyric quality to his music that has overshadowed the grotesque touches so prominent in his early compositions. He kept, however, the childlike sense of humor so delightfully apparent in the musical fairy tale for children, *Peter and the Wolf*. In this score each character is represented by an instrument in the orchestra: the Wolf by the French horns, Peter's grandfather by the bassoon, etc.

Dmitri Shostakovich, born in Russia in 1906, ranks with Stravinsky and Prokofiev as one of the three most important composers Russia has produced in modern times. Aside from his undoubted talent, Shostakovich is interesting as an example of a creative artist adapting himself to political and social changes, and to the tastes of a mass public.

He composed his First Symphony when he was nineteen, and through its performance a year later he attracted immediate attention. Here was a work that had ingenious melodies and novel rhythms; it was modern enough to be interesting, and academic enough to be agreeable and understood. In a way it was neoclassic, for it was direct and to the point, with a structural design that was easily followed.

A year later Shostakovich presented his Second Symphony, written for the tenth anniversary of the Soviet Republic. This did not meet with the success of the First Symphony. Next, the composer wrote an opera, *The Nose,* which satirized an important government official. In its score Shostakovich became complex, and used atonal patterns. The opera was produced at Leningrad in 1930, and was assailed by the Russian Association of Proletarian Composers as a product of "bourgeois decadence."

The Third Symphony, like the Second, had political significance. Modeled after the Ninth Symphony of Beethoven, it ended with a choral movement in the form of a May Day Hymn. This symphony was followed by two more ballets, both of them satirical, with indictments of non-Soviet peoples. Then came a most significant work, a second opera, *Lady Macbeth of the District of Mzensk*. In spite of a highly suggestive interlude, which was eliminated from Russian productions of the opera, *Lady Macbeth* enjoyed a vogue in Russia and in other countries. Official indictment, however, in the form of an article in *Pravda,* condemned the work as theatrically vulgar and "musically formalistic."

This article was followed by another, in the same periodical, which attacked a Shostakovich ballet, *The Limpid Stream,* as a frivolous and oversimplified essay on the subject of collective farming. It looked as though official disfavor would bring an end to Shostakovich's brilliant career. To prevent this, the young composer accomplished a complete change of creative style, and was genius enough to do it successfully. He withdrew a fourth symphony, and started writing a fifth, which was performed late in 1937, and achieved tremendous success. Shostakovich again became the favorite composer of the Russian people, and the musical spokesman for the Soviet government.

During the summer of 1942 (July 19), the NBC Symphony Orchestra, under Toscanini, gave the first American performance to Shostakovich's Seventh Symphony. This was one of the first major works to be inspired by the Second World War, and it was composed, for the most part, near one of the fighting fronts. The composer began it in June, 1941, and wrote much of the score in Leningrad while he was engaged in watching for fires and in other defense activities of the besieged city.

The symphony is dedicated "to our struggle against Fascism, to our future victory, to my native city, Leningrad." It is a lengthy work; the American première ran about an hour and a quarter, and critical opinion agreed upon the sincerity of the symphony and the imposing effect of the climaxes, but observed that it was marred by unevenness of outline, resulting perhaps from the circumstances of its composition. There could hardly have been opportunity, under the conditions, for the composer to sift and weigh the value of his material, and subject it to his own stiff criticism.

Some other rationalization must be contrived for the meretricious Eighth Symphony of 1945; likewise the Ninth of a year later. The Tenth, however, needs none. It is a work of high art at high compression, and devoid of any kow-towing to bureaucracy.

The neoclassic movement has touched composers of widely separated styles and ideals. In Spain, we find Manuel de Falla composing a Harpsichord Concerto (1923–26), for harpsichord (or piano) and flute, oboe, clarinet, violin, and 'cello. De Falla is steeped in the Spanish tradition, and through his own individuality has brought a fusion of his nation's past and present.

In Italy, Alfredo Casella was at one time violently assailed for his modernism, and his *Elegia Eroica,* dedicated to the war dead, provoked a riot when it was performed at Rome in 1917. Casella worked out a polytonal style that was lacking in all the chromaticisms of the romanticists.[5] More recently his Concerto for String Quartet, composed in 1923–24, reverted to an Italian classicism, even though it employed an extended tonal system. In 1926 he followed the example of Stravinsky's *Pulcinella* by writing a work for piano and

[5] See pages 33–34.

orchestra called *Scarlattiana,* based on themes of Scarlatti.

The Swiss-American Ernest Bloch (1880——) has composed two Concerti Grossi for strings and piano obbligato, both full of new ideas in old patterns. Falla, Casella, and Bloch have already been mentioned for their impressionism (Chapter 5).

The two Americans most closely identified with neoclassicism are the lately more neoromantic Walter Piston (1894——) and the more and more granitic Roger Sessions (1896——). In spite of his advanced harmonic combinations, Piston is always direct and to the point; he respects convention in the formal design of his structure, and he is exceedingly fond of imitative counterpoint, and the canon and fugue of the eighteenth century. His music for the ballet, *The Incredible Flutist,* is delightful in its simplicity and this quality also marks his more ambitious productions. The Fourth Symphony (1952) was perhaps his most personal statement and certainly his boldest; three of its four movements sweep to climaxes of stunning resonance.

Piston is a native of Maine and is head of the music department at Harvard University.

Sessions has acknowledged Stravinsky's influence, but he insists that he does not belong to any "school" or limited group of stylists. In 1927 he announced: "I reject any kind of dogma or platform. I am not trying to write 'modern,' 'American,' or 'neo-classic' music. I am seeking always and only the coherent and living expression of my musical ideas." [6] In spite of this disclaimer, there is in Sessions' mature work an orthodox feeling for form; his String Quartet most certainly labels him as a composer with the ideals of a classicist. He is by nature a perfectionist, which is perhaps responsible for his relatively small number of works. In the

[6] Quoted by Nicolas Slonimsky in *American Composers on American Music.* Stanford University Press; copyright 1933 by the Board of Trustees of Leland Stanford Junior University.

1927 statement he declared: "I dislike rhetoric, overemphasis, vulgarity, but at the same time believe that perfection in art consists in a sort of equilibrium which can be neither defined nor counterfeited."

In his Three Chorales for Organ and in his Piano Sonata, Sessions shows his love for perfection in design and structure, and sometimes the manner in which he expresses his ideas is more significant than the ideas themselves. He has also several symphonies, a Violin Concerto, three dirges for orchestra, and numerous other works that have enjoyed critically (if not popularly) successful performances. Like Piston, he is a teacher of composition. For many years he has been associated with Princeton University.

It was there, in 1955, that New York critics ventured to hear his one-act opera, *The Trial of Lucullus*. The consensus was not favorable, at least as far as the work's stage-worthiness was concerned. His *Idyll of Theocritus,* for dramatic soprano and orchestra, was more cordially received the following year. The Second Quartet of 1952 probably was his most outstanding work of this period, although his early programatic piece, *The Black Maskers,* remained Sessions' only representation in the standard repertory.

Roy Harris, born in Oklahoma in 1898, is one of the most picturesque figures among our creative musicians. Like Sessions and a few other iconoclasts, he is not easy to classify. He is polytonal whenever he finds that combined tonalities answer his purpose; he is rarely, if ever, atonal; his intense Americanism, with its racy flavor of the Southwest, gives his work a highly nationalistic character. He is, however, very much the neoclassicist in his attempt to adapt old forms to present-day needs. Harris makes no compromise whatever with the conservative elements in his audiences. He never tries to write music that will be easy for traditionally conditioned ears to listen to; much of his work is difficult and disconcerting at first hearing. His dissonances are uncompromising and caustic, and his structure is involved and complex in spite of his neoclassic leanings.

Behind all of Harris' works there is an idealism and a philosophy that motivate his underlying principles and crystallize his thought. The explanation he advanced for his First Symphony is characteristic. In its three movements, he said, he tried "to capture the mood of adventure and physical exuberance"; then to show "the pathos which seems to underlie all human existence"; and finally, to catch "the mood of a positive will to power and action." The long list of Harris' works includes eight symphonies (the Third of 1938 remains his finest achievement), an Orchestral Suite, a Piano Sonata, several string quartets, a Sextet, and a *Symphony for Voices*.

Yet, while Harris can attain such enviable heights in some of his works, his facility for mass production has led him into many pitfalls. He may with justice pride himself on the fact that his vogue has not been achieved by concessions to the public; he has punished its ears cruelly on occasion and it comes back for more, but a careful review of the repeat performances shows that his actual hold on the public rests on relatively few of his compositions.

Three other composers, highly disparate in their aesthetics, are due consideration. Paul Creston (New York City, 1906) has written five symphonies, all of them melodious, surcharged with intensity, and given to personal rhetoric at the expense of form. This has not militated against their substantial and growing acceptance among the broader public. Samuel Barber (West Chester, Pa., 1910) used to be widely heard but the level of his mature effort has not fulfilled the promise of his early *Adagio for Strings*, the two *Essays for Orchestra*, and the magnificent *Symphony in One Movement* of 1936. William Schuman (New York City, 1910) has given us, in his Third Symphony of 1941 and Sixth Symphony of 1948, two of the most impressive utterances of the twentieth century. His fusion of the several chromatic styles (*i. e.,* out of Schoenberg) is effected by a linear classicism no less strong than the personality that is its motor force.

9

MUSIC FOR
EVERYDAY USE
—GEBRAUCHSMUSIK

CLOSELY ALLIED WITH NEOCLASSICISM, PRINCIPALLY BECAUSE
it also tends to simplify music, is *Gebrauchsmusik*, tagged
with a German label since it originated in the post-War
Germany of the 1920's. Literally translated, the term means
"music for use," and that is exactly what it is.

In the mid-1920's, a number of composers became aware
of the fact that their audience of educated music lovers was
pitifully small, and that they were completely out of touch
with the vast potential audience of young people and of
older persons who were not in the habit of going to concerts. Perhaps the radio and sound pictures had something
to do with it, but at any rate a few musicians felt that if they
could write music that would be played in places besides the
concert halls and grand opera houses, they would have a
wider market for their product.

Consequently, they decided to compose what might be
termed practical, or workaday, music, which would either
be adapted to the needs of musical amateurs, or written for
some specific purpose outside the accepted channels of symphony orchestras or opera companies. The *Gebrauchsmusik*
movement has taken two directions: the first, developing
music for amateurs to perform—operettas and cantatas for
school children, instrumental pieces for school and college
orchestras, and works in which the audience participates by
singing some of the choruses and songs. The other type of
Gebrauchsmusik is for performance by professionals, but

intended for a wide audience: incidental music for sound
pictures and plays and for radio, light operas that have popular appeal, and most recently, operas for television. There
has also been written music that has political and social
significance in a changing world.

It is generally believed that the *Gebrauchsmusik* movement had its impetus from the German composer, Paul
Hindemith, in the years around 1927. Hindemith, born in
1895 at Hanau, near Frankfort, is a composer who started
his career with a thoroughly practical and wide experience.
At the age of thirteen he had mastered the violin, and played
widely in orchestras at motion picture houses, musical comedy theaters, in dance bands, and, finally, in symphony
orchestras. He studied at Hoch's Conservatory in Frankfort,
and from 1915 to 1923 was concertmaster at the Frankfort
Opera. He also founded a string quartet. Finally he became
professor at the Hochschule in Berlin, where he remained
until the displeasure of the Third Reich caused him to make
his home in the United States.

As a composer, Hindemith showed from the start his practical experience as an orchestral musician, as well as a sense
of humor that could be either playful or ironical. At first
his music reflected the influence of such composers as Brahms
and Max Reger, but he eventually put aside romantic ten-
dencies and turned to a style closely allied to neoclassicism,
reflecting the detached, impersonal point of view that he had
consciously adopted.

Hindemith's works for the accustomed audience of music
lovers cover a wide range, for he has been prolific. There
are several operas, of which *Mathis der Maler* is the best
known; an orchestral symphony from the same opera; a
Concerto for Orchestra; the popular ballet score, *The Four
Temperaments;* the virtuosic *Symphonic Metamorphosis on
Themes by Weber;* a powerful symphony entitled *Harmonie*

der Welt; five works for chamber orchestra, which he calls *Kammermusik;* four string quartets; two string trios; a number of sonatas for various instruments and combinations; three sonatas and a Suite for Piano, as well as a considerable list of piano pieces, songs, and choral works. Although Hindemith has at times departed so far from fixed tonalities as to omit key signatures, he has never been an actual atonalist. In recent years his feeling for tonality has reasserted itself, and whatever he writes nowadays has a distinct tonal center.

In 1927 Hindemith summarized his attitude regarding practical uses for music in the following words: "It is to be regretted that in general so little relationship exists today between the producers and the consumers of music. A composer should write today only if he knows for what purpose he is writing. The days of composing for the sake of composing are perhaps gone forever. On the other hand, the demand for music is so great that composer and consumer ought most emphatically to come at last to an understanding." [1]

The works that Hindemith has composed for his new audience cover a wide field. First there were a number of pieces for mechanical instruments; then came music to accompany a motion picture film, *Felix the Cat,* to be played by a mechanical organ. These works are still in manuscript, but in 1927 Hindemith published a number of pieces for amateurs: *Spielmusik* (*Music to Play*) for Strings, Flutes, and Oboes; a group of Songs for Singing Groups; and an educational work for violin ensembles. After these came a variety of music to sing or play, designed for use by amateurs or music lovers. Some of them call for audience participation through community singing. *Let's Build a Town,* composed in 1931, is a play with music for children.

[1] Quoted by Willi Reich in an article on Hindemith in the *Musical Quarterly,* October, 1931.

Motion pictures naturally provided an attractive vehicle for the kind of music Hindemith wanted to write, and in his work at the Hochschule in Berlin he conducted a Film-Music Studio. Here he put his pupils to work studying the mechanical processes of film production. They learned to synchronize musical measures with sections of film, and composed music to old films, cut and fitted for the purpose.

Kurt Weill (1900–1950) was another German exponent of *Gebrauchsmusik*. Early in life he set himself the task of developing a new type of musical play. His first important experiment in this direction was called *Die Dreigroschenoper* (*The Three-Penny Opera*), which took for its pattern Gay's famous *Beggar's Opera*. In later years he lived in America, where he composed incidental music for plays as well as scores for sound pictures and several musical comedies. In 1933 his two-act operetta, *Der Jasager,* intended for performance for young people, was produced by the Music School of the Henry Street Settlement in New York. He composed incidental music for Max Reinhardt's New York production of Franz Werfel's play, *The Eternal Road,* and in 1936 he supplied a musical background for Paul Green's *Johnny Johnson.* He collaborated with Maxwell Anderson in writing the musical comedy that starred Walter Huston, *Knickerbocker Holiday* (1938), and he composed the score for the New York World's Fair transportation pageant, *Railroads on Parade* (1939–40). Among his late works, the folk opera, *Down in the Valley* (1948), has proved its resilience as a vehicle for workshop and repertory companies alike. His *Lady in the Dark* and *Lost in the Stars* of the forties were of exceptional quality for their Broadway *genre;* likewise his incidental music for the Elmer Rice play, *Street Scene* (1947).

Ernst Křenek, born in Vienna, 1900, and now living in the United States, has been known both as a neoclassicist and as an atonalist, having adopted Schoenberg's twelve-tone technique and altered it to suit his own purposes. He achieved his greatest fame, however, by a work that was closely allied with the *Gebrauchsmusik* movement, an opera that incorporated American jazz patterns, entitled *Jonny spielt auf.* This work was rejected by several leading theaters in Germany, but was finally produced at Leipzig in 1927. It scored such a tremendous success that it was eventually performed in more than one hundred cities and translated into eighteen languages. In 1929 it was produced at the Metropolitan in New York.

Both Weill and Křenek succeeded in giving large audiences an art music they can comprehend. In their stage works they substituted for the high-flown aria songs in the musical comedy manner, some of them in the jazz vein. On the whole, they succeeded in producing an art product that had popular appeal, and which successfully avoided being "arty" or overprecious.

Marc Blitzstein, born in Philadelphia in 1905, has shown the influence of Kurt Weill by developing a type of stage entertainment that may conceivably develop into an indigenous form of opera. He employs a type of performer who might be termed a singing actor rather than an acting singer, and he provides his characters with dialogue and lyrics of his own writing that are convincing and realistic. In 1937 Blitzstein's satiric light opera, *The Cradle Will Rock,* was produced at the Mercury Theatre in New York. It had a successful run then and has been successfully revived. This was followed by a similar work, *No for an Answer,* as well as a half-hour radio opera, *I've Got the Tune.*

In the wake of World War II, in 1946, Blitzstein gave us *The Airborne Symphony,* which has not endured. The year following, his "musical drama," *Regina,* had a moderate success (some of which was attributed to the merits of Lillian

Hellman's play, *The Little Foxes*); in the fifties it was given several times at New York City Center, but never with signal success.

Blitzstein has burdened some of his works with left-wing theories that lend them the function of class struggle propaganda. This limits their appeal, but it provides them a purpose which is sincere and direct.

Many other American composers have interested themselves in the new market for their music, and have come to realize that the millions of children who are nowadays receiving instrumental as well as vocal training in the schools need good music written especially for them. Thus we find such composers as Douglas Moore (1893——) composing an operetta for amateur and school groups, *The Headless Horseman,* first produced in Bronxville, New York, in 1937.

Moore has become, indeed, one of America's most important composers for the lyric theater, a medium for which his amiable aesthetic is ideally suited. His 1939 "folk opera," *The Devil and Daniel Webster,* has been a favorite from the first; in 1953 it was revived for a summer-long run. His *Giants in the Earth* (1951) did not achieve the same measure of success; the composer said later that he felt he had overemphasized dramatic action at the expense of arias and other operatic formalities. By all odds the finest of Moore's operas is *The Ballad of Baby Doe* (1956); the libretto by John Latouche was based on the incredible but true story of Colorado's silver king, Horace Tabor, and his two wives.

High school orchestras are a particularly tempting market, for there are thousands of them, and since they are made up of twentieth-century youngsters, they are interested in twentieth-century music.

The sound pictures, too, have need for serious composers as well as for the tunesmiths who write songs for the so-called "musicals" and "revues." Producers have found that musical background is essential for drama, to blend and tie together moods and atmosphere, and to establish continuity and contrast between episodes and scenes. Werner Janssen, George Antheil, Louis Gruenberg, Franz Waxman are but a few of the prominent American or Americanized composers whom Hollywood has called upon for originally composed scores to accompany films.

Radio and television have proved to be fertile fields for experiment. Many of their presentations, particularly in the operatic field, have been adaptations of standard works, but the leading networks have encouraged (through contests and outright commissions) the writing of original material. Among the latter have been Gian-Carlo Menotti's *The Old Maid and the Thief, Amahl and the Night Visitors,* and *The Saint of Bleecker Street;* Louis Gruenberg's *Green Mansions,* Vittorio Giannini's *Beauty and the Beast,* Randall Thompson's *Solomon and Balkis,* Leonard Bernstein's *Trouble in Tahiti,* Mark Bucci's *The 13 Clocks,* Norman Dello Joio's *The Trial at Rouen,* and the *Griffelkin* of Lukas Foss. In addition, dozens of instrumental works have been composed with radio or TV requirements in mind.

Music like the foregoing has been on the whole contemporary in spirit, making liberal use of the newest idioms. The mass audience factor has rarely caused these composers to take refuge in conservatism as such. Rather, it has challenged their ingenuity. One result now taking shape is the *genre* of TV opera—a sort of small-scale form akin to chamber opera but far more dependent on smooth continuity, for a few static minutes will twirl hundreds of thousands of receiver dials.

At this juncture it would be appropriate to mention the enormous contribution that opera workshops the nation over have made to our reawakened interest in lyric theater. In the past decade alone, countless works have been composed expressly for workshop production (and doubtless with an eye to TV adaptation). Virtually every college and university today boasts an opera workshop, and certain of them have outdistanced even the metropolitan centers in their willingness to mount the most challenging works. The currently popular Bavarian composer Carl Orff (b. 1895), for example, was unknown in the United States until his "scenic cantata" *Carmina Burana* was introduced on a midwestern campus.

Aaron Copland, born in Brooklyn, New York, in 1900, has been a prominent leader among American composers in the movement to compose art works that are practical for performance by a wider circle than professional musicians, or are designed for the constantly increasing audience of listeners outside the concert halls—on the radio and in the theater. In his fine book, *Our New Music*,[2] Copland gives an interesting account of himself and of his aims. In the chapter, "Composer from Brooklyn," he explains: "During these years [1930–1935] I began to feel an increasing dissatisfaction with the relations of the music-loving public and the living composer. The old 'special public' of the modern music concerts had fallen away, and the conventional concert public continued apathetic or indifferent to anything but the established classics. It seemed to me that we composers were in danger of working in a vacuum. Moreover, an entirely new public for music had grown up around the radio and phonograph. It made no sense to ignore them and to continue writing as if they did not exist. I felt it was worth the effort to see if I couldn't say what I had to say in the simplest possible terms."

Before he came to this decision, Copland had already established himself as one of our leading contemporary American composers, a man whose music was in tune with modern thought and present-day developments. Trained by Rubin

[2] New York: Whittlesey House, 1941.

Goldmark in New York and Nadia Boulanger in Paris, he was schooled in conventional theory but was also aware of twentieth-century changes in musical patterns. His first important works were a Symphony for Organ and Orchestra, a Suite for Orchestra, *Music for the Theatre,* and a Piano Concerto in which he employed jazz elements in symphonic texture. At that time he felt that jazz was something the serious composer could use to advantage but, as he explains in his book, he found that in the concerto he had done all he could with the idiom, considering its limited emotional scope. "True," he wrote, "it was an easy way to be an American in musical terms, but all American music could not possibly be confined to two dominant jazz moods: the 'blues' and the snappy number." [3]

In line with the neoclassic movement as well as toward a music that is practical and workaday, Copland has aimed at a simpler music, works that are "more spare in sonority, more lean in texture." Striving for an "imposed simplicity," he has composed his highly popular *El Salón México,* a musical picture of a Mexican dance hall, based on Mexican tunes; an opera for high school children to perform: *The Second Hurricane;* a full-length opera, *The Tender Land* (which failed); orchestral works for radio performance, a ballet, *Billy the Kid,* composed for the Ballet Caravan, using cowboy songs; and several scores for sound pictures: *The City, Of Mice and Men,* and *Our Town.* His massively sonorous Third Symphony of 1946 was a considerable departure from all this; Serge Koussevitzky hailed it as "the greatest American symphony" but it has not yet gained repertory standing. Fortunately, it has been recorded.

Another American who aims at simplification and who shuns the grand manner is Virgil Thomson, born in Kansas City in 1896, educated at Harvard and in Paris, and a resi-

[3] *Ibid.*

dent of the French capital from 1925 to the thirties. In 1940 he succeeded the late Lawrence Gilman as music critic of the New York *Herald Tribune,* serving until 1954.

Thomson first came into prominence when his setting of Gertrude Stein's *Four Saints in Three Acts* was presented in New York in 1934. Here was something that was novelty plus, and many who went to laugh and scoff came away enchanted. The libretto purposely made no sense whatever. It consisted entirely of words strung along with no apparent meaning, just because the author liked the sound of them. The musical setting, however, seemed somehow to make sense of all this nonsense. Aaron Copland has written a shrewd analysis of Thomson's score. "He gave the words," writes Copland, "their true speech inflection just as if their sense meaning were continuously understandable, in its emotional intention. The trick lay in making his musical emotion entirely serious and entirely unambiguous in its purpose—practically without regard to the thing said. That is what gave the opera its amusement and charm. One must add to this the inverted shock provided by Thomsons's antimodernism. Swinging away from whatever might jar or confuse the ear, he wrote with a simplicity unprecedented among contemporary composers, often confining himself to the most rudimentary scales and harmonic progressions. There may have been a minimum of music in *Four Saints,* but in combination with the unique costumes and stage setting . . . , the all-Negro cast, the melodious prose of the libretto, and the fresh scenic action, an original theater work was created that made all other American musical stage pieces seem dull by comparison." [4]

In many respects, Thomson is the American counterpart of Erik Satie, the French satirist. The similarity is more one of spirit than of the actual music each has written, but never-

[4] In *Our New Music. Op. cit.*

theless the attitudes of the two composers are largely the same. Thomson is an avowed admirer of Satie, and has claimed that Satie invented the only twentieth-century musical aesthetic in the musical world.

Just as some composers are termed neoclassic, Thomson might be termed neoromantic, for while he shuns the towering and lofty flights of the German romanticists, he never hesitates to become sentimental, even though he may at times have his tongue in his cheek. For thematic material, in addition to original melodies of his own, he employs old waltz tunes, hymn tunes, French folk songs, snatches of popular songs, ancient Gregorian chants—anything that will suit his purpose.

In his belief that music's prime function is to be entertaining, and to provide relaxation, Thomson is closely allied with the *Gebrauchsmusik* movement. In this direction he has furnished scores for motion pictures, particularly the documentary films: *The River, The Plow that Broke the Plains,* and *The Louisiana Story;* and has composed a highly entertaining ballet score entitled *Filling Station.* He has also written some chamber music and a symphony, but his outstanding gift seems to be in the direction of vocal works.

Thomson's most recent opera, *The Mother of Us All,* was given in première at New York in 1947 and revived as recently as 1956. Like *Four Saints,* its text is by Gertrude Stein; unlike *Four Saints,* its story line is thoroughly comprehensible (all about Susan B. Anthony's fight for woman suffrage). Musically, the work is ingenious, engaging, and, in retrospect, endearing. One suspects that this is Thomson's masterpiece.

FROM PLAIN
SONG TO JAZZ—
A STORY OF RHYTHMS

THUS FAR ONLY PASSING REFERENCE HAS BEEN MADE TO THE rhythmic features of modern music, to their increasing freedom and complexity. These things have been seemingly neglected, not because they are unimportant, but rather because they are so important that they require a chapter to themselves.

Without rhythm there is no music; the entire contour of any melody is determined by the regular or irregular succession of beats in which it is played or sung. If you want an example of what rhythm can do to a series of tones, go to the piano and play the scale of C downward, starting at the C an octave above middle C. Play it slowly and regularly, and all you have is the descending scale of C major.

Then play it in the following manner, and you have the opening phrase of the Christmas hymn, *Joy to the World:*

Rhythm existed before melody; it was present in the universe before man came into being—in the movement of the planets and the recurrence of seasons. It is the basis of vital functions—beating of the heart, breathing, as well as of such conscious activities as walking and speech. Even the cries of animals are rhythmic.

Although melody cannot exist without some sort of rhythm,

rhythm is able to stand on its own feet without melody, or even without musical tone. Drum beats are merely sound, except in cases where the drums produce a tone of definite pitch, yet to many peoples, particularly primitive races, the rhythms of a drum are completely satisfying. Primitives are often found to be interested in little more than rhythm, and their drum beats are more involved and complex than the rhythms of the most advanced music of cultivated musicians.

Since rhythm is such an important factor in all music, it is inevitable that rhythmic patterns have changed and developed as music has been adapted to the needs and demands of various eras. And just as other elements of music have changed through the centuries to reflect the background of their time, so have rhythms interpreted and expressed the contemporary life and thought of nations and peoples. It is significant that times of stress, or war, or panic have generally produced music with exciting rhythms. Similarly, as people have grown more sophisticated, their music has been marked by subtler, more complex rhythms. In this, however, they have often reverted to the expression of their barbaric ancestors.

Rhythms may be generally classified in two major groups: those that are measured, or strict, and those that are free. Measured rhythms are marked by regular repetitions of accent and beat and length of phrase. The opening stanza from Gray's *Elegy* is an example of measured rhythm:

> The curfew tolls the knell of parting day,
> The lowing herd winds slowly o'er the lea,
> The ploughman homeward plods his weary way,
> And leaves the world to darkness and to me.

Modern poets use freer rhythms, but in doing so they are not as modern as they seem. They are actually reverting to

early practice, and if we want specimens of free rhythm
we need merely turn to the pages of the King James version
of the Bible:

The Lord is my shepherd; I shall not want.
He maketh me to lie down in green pastures: he leadeth
  me beside the still waters.
He restoreth my soul: he leadeth me in the paths of right-
  eousness for his name's sake.

The Puritans sang the Psalms to tunes in measured
rhythm, so they had to re-translate them to fit their purpose.
In the *Bay Psalm Book*, first printed at Cambridge, Massachusetts, in 1640, the 23d Psalm was rendered thus:

> The Lord to mee a shepheard is,
>   want therefore shall not I.
> Hee in the folds of tender-grasse,
>   doth cause mee downe to lie:
> To waters calme me gently leads
>   Restore my soule doth hee:
> He doth in paths of righteousness:
>   for his names sake leade mee.

In mediaeval plain song the rhythm was free, and the repetition of beats followed the accents of the Latin text.
Consequently, plain song is not divided into measures, and
has no regular repetition of strong and weak beats. This
freedom of accent has been preserved to a certain extent in
the recitatives of opera and oratorio.

The conception of measured rhythm in music, and its notation in symbols, resulted from the application of prosody to
music, for rhythm is to music what meter is to poetry. The
chorale took the place of the Gregorian chant (plain song),

and became characteristic of the reformed church of Germany and the Lutheran movement. Luther realized that his followers did not understand the Latin texts of the Roman Church, and to encourage congregational singing he adapted folk songs, which were regularly phrased, to metrical verses. One of the most famous of these is *Ein feste Burg:*

> A mighty fortress is our God,
> A bulwark never failing;
> Our helper He, amid the flood
> Of mortal ills prevailing.

In the chorales the phrasing is regular, and each phrase is followed by a definite pause. Bach made settings of more than four hundred chorales, and they became the foundation on which the art music of later centuries was built. They affected the structure not only of vocal music but of instrumental music as well, and we find the themes of instrumental works, well into the nineteenth century, falling into measured rhythm and definite phrases that answered and echoed each other like the meters and rhymes of a Longfellow poem. In measured music, phrases fall into patterns of two or four measures in length, separated by pauses that correspond to the punctuation of written language.

The human ear by nature conceives rhythm in units of two or three fundamental beats. Walking and marching are based on a unit of two; while dancing has for its basis either twos (four and eight, of course, are merely multiples of two) or threes. Musical time signatures, therefore, are generally derived from such units as: $\frac{2}{4}$, $\frac{4}{4}$, $\frac{2}{2}$, or $\frac{3}{4}$, $\frac{6}{4}$, $\frac{3}{2}$, etc.

In seeking freedom from the restraints of eighteenth-century music, the romantic composers liberated their rhythms as well as their harmonies and formal structures.

Many of them broke away from the phrase and period structure in their melodies, and wrote longer-breathed themes
that were more flexible and pliant. Sometimes they would
shift the meter from two to three within the limits of a single
measure.

Modern composers have learned to extend basic units to
groupings not divisible by two or three. Tchaikovsky made
a start in this direction by writing the second movement of
his *Pathétique* symphony in ⁵⁄₄ rhythm. Each measure was
a unit of five, or a combination of two and three.

The pattern of five in Tchaikovsky's symphony remained
unchanged throughout the entire movement, but later composers, notably Stravinsky, have indulged in rapid and constant changes of time signature. In *Le Sacre du printemps*
the rhythmic indications often change with each measure:
⁴⁄₄, ³⁄₄, ⁴⁄₄, ²⁄₄, ³⁄₄, or even ⁵⁄₄, ⁷⁄₄, ⁶⁄₄, ⁵⁄₄.

It is not only in changing and alternating basic rhythms
that music has become complex, it has also combined rhythms
to produce polyrhythms, just as combining two or more keys
produces polytonality. Combined rhythms are not a new
device; Beethoven combined two and three in his Rondo in
C major:

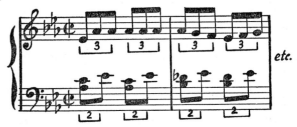

In this passage the right hand plays three beats while the
left plays two, in effect. Chopin used a two against three
figure in his A flat Etude:

In his *Fantaisie impromptu* Chopin imposed four on three:

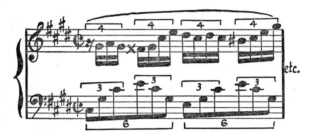

These specimens of polyrhythms are comparatively straightforward, but modern composers use combinations that are far more complex. At one point in *Le Sacre*, Stravinsky superimposes an alternating 2/4 and 5/8 on an underlying 3/8. Charles Ives gains a novel polyrhythmic effect in *Washington's Birthday*, the opening movement of his symphony *Holidays*. At one point the orchestra changes from a rapid allegro to a slow pace. The viola, however, is unaware of the change and continues at the rapid tempo. At another place, when the orchestra is playing at a brisk speed, the flute feels that the pace should be a trifle faster, and as a result, finishes ahead of the others. The effect is that of a village parade where the marchers have difficulty in keeping step with their fellows.

To primitive peoples such combinations of rhythms would prove child's play. It is no feat at all for an African musician to sing in one rhythm, beat his drums in another, and stamp his feet in a third. And if you want to hear really complex rhythms, listen to the Angel record, *Music of India.*

Nationalism in music has resulted in characteristic rhythms. The Spanish composers—Falla, Albéniz, Granados, and others—have incorporated in their works the peculiar rhythms of Spanish folk songs and dances. The Hungarian Rhapsodies of Liszt have the rhythmic as well as the melodic irregularities of Hungarian Gypsy music. The waltzes of Johann Strauss are distinguished by the subtle accenting of the second beat in the triple waltz measure—a typically Viennese device. And all composers who have drawn on the folk songs of the American Negro have emphasized their syncopation.

We hear a great deal about syncopation these days, and it is often looked upon as something new, developed solely for our present-day jazz and swing. Syncopation is truly an essential feature of American dance music, but as a rhythmic device it is very old, and by no means confined to any nation or any single period in the history of music. It was known to the religious composers of the Middle Ages; Bach used accenting that would seem novel trickery in the hands of a Broadway tunesmith; Beethoven was almost jazzy in the syncopation of the second movement of the *Moonlight Sonata;* while Schumann wrote syncopated rhythms on almost every page of his music.

Syncopation results from shifting the rhythmic accent from the strong beats of a measure to the normally weak, or unaccented, beats. In a Sousa march, the accents fall on the normally strong beats; the tempo, and the accents, fit the swing and rhythmic cadence of marching feet: *one,* two, *three,* four; *one,* two, *three,* four; etc. The first and third

beats of a group of four are the normally strong beats. Two
and four are the secondary, or weak, beats.

Similarly, in measured verse, the strong beats are the
ones that are normally accented:

Lives' of great' men all' remind' us
We' can make' our lives' sublime'

If we should sing the first line of this quotation from Longfellow to the principal theme of Liszt's *Hungarian Fantasy*
we would have an entirely different accenting:

Lives of great men all re - mind us

Thus, placing the strong accents where weak beats are expected results in syncopation. The accents may be anticipated
or delayed, as long as they fall at points where they are not
normally expected.

Although syncopation is found in the works of Bach, Beethoven, and Schumann, modern syncopation in the twentieth
century comes from a more primitive source. It derives from
the songs of the American Negro, from his spirituals and
work songs. These melodies are of vague origin, and have
been influenced to a great degree by the songs of the white
man that the Negro heard in this country. Nevertheless,
the African heritage of the Negro, and the frenetic rhythms
and syncopations of his primitive ancestors, have indisputably
determined the peculiar rhythmic characteristics of American Negro folk songs.

Up to the latter part of the nineteenth century these
rhythmic characteristics were left to the Negroes themselves;
even Stephen Foster's "Ethiopian" songs were not synco-

pated, and few of the "Negro" minstrel songs, written by white men, had any rhythmic departures from normal accenting. It was with the "coon songs" and the "ragtime" of the 1890's that Negro syncopation came into our popular music, and there began the development of a type of music, culminating in jazz and swing, that is the result of Negro music shaped by American life and surroundings and developed by white men as much as by Negroes.

Ragtime, which came into use about 1895, was comparatively straightforward. It was characterized by a so-called rhythmic snap (sometimes called the Scotch snap because it is found also in the folk songs of Scotland) which is produced by the false accenting we have already discussed: the accent falling on a weak rather than on a strong beat.

The syncopated pattern of such early specimens as *At a Georgia Camp Meeting* and the *Maple Leaf Rag* was regular

AT A GEORGIA CAMP MEETING

and consistent, and not at all involved or complex. The vogue of ragtime, however, was responsible for the later, more complicated jazz developments that have been a direct outgrowth of the early attempts at syncopation.

Nobody knows who invented jazz, nor who gave it its name. It was not familiar to the general public until 1915, but it had probably existed among the Negroes for some time before that. It is generally believed that it originated in

New Orleans, for a couple of dance bands moved from that city to Chicago in 1914 and started a vogue for the new type of dance music, a fashion that spread rapidly to other centers of the country. Since then jazz has provided the pattern on which most American dance music has been based.

Jazz music has three distinguishing features. One is the instrumentation of its orchestra—saxophones; muted trumpets; wailing, squealing clarinets; novel and terrifying percussion devices. Another characteristic consists in definite melodic and harmonic traits—"blue" notes, dissonant chords, etc. The third, and most important, feature of jazz is found in its many rhythms. Jazz rhythms are based on syncopation, but a far more sophisticated and involved syncopation than has been used in earlier music except, perhaps, among primitive tribes in various parts of the world. Since jazz music is primarily intended for dancing, or some sort of bodily movement, it sets in motion an underlying $\frac{4}{4}$ beat that continues throughout the length of a piece. This, fundamentally, is the same basic pattern as that of a Sousa march; but while the Sousa march actually gives the accents you expect, jazz dodges them, and gives you an irresistible impulse to fill them in for yourself.

The obvious accents are avoided in several ways. Sometimes they are anticipated, or delayed, and on other occasions they are almost completely suppressed. The most ingenious and complicated method is the setting up of conflicting accents, resulting in polyrhythms. The most accepted method of using conflicting rhythms is having the bass parts beat a regular, monotonous four-four meter, while the upper parts, and the melody, employ counterrhythms and dodge the normal, expected accents.

In George Gershwin's *I Got Rhythm* the bass maintains a compound two figure, which is really four, and the melody enters on the off beat (the second half of the first beat).

By using dotted quarter notes (which are equal in duration to one and a half quarter notes) the melody shifts its accent so that it falls with the accent of the bass only once in each phrase:

Jazz music mostly follows two main streams, more or less distinct from each other. One comes from the folk art of Negro musicians, and the shouting and crooning of the untrained colored singer. The other branch is more commercialized and standardized: the Tin-Pan Alley product, which comes primarily from the same source, but which is written out in all its instrumentation by an arranger, so that the performers need merely follow the notes in the music.

The first type of jazz allows, and demands, spontaneous improvisation by the performers. The printed notes may be before the players, but they are largely ignored, and each musician improvises freely on the harmonic basis of an agreed-upon tune. The result abounds in cross rhythms, highly dissonant counterpoint, and ingenious melodic development. All of this produced a musical cult. It gathered to its ranks millions of fans and devotees who worshiped what became known as "swing" music and later, in a slightly more intellectualized manifestation, as "bebop"—the so-called "rock-'n'-roll" variant being its atavistic *reductio ad absurdum*. Perhaps no further description is needed for the reader who listens to the radio and the "juke-box" or spends his evenings at night clubs.

But some clarification of the more recently fashionable terminology would be in order, especially as regards the wake (no pun intended) of "bebop." The latter had its origins around 1940, when jazzmen began to toy with such long-available phenomena as the chord of the ninth with a flatted fifth, and when the four-to-the-bar beat began to be discarded in favor of more subtle rhythms. Coteries gathered around each new nonconformist in turn, giving the orthodox "Dixieland" practitioners a chance to broaden the base of their appeal (which remains wide despite the now formula-pat commercialization). At the same time, big-band swing began cautiously to take on certain of the innovations tried and tested by the *avant-garde*.

By 1950 there had evolved what its dedicated adherents call "cool" jazz, subsequently better known (if not better described) as "progressive." Essentially introverted, this style tends to relatively low decibel output, minimal personnel, precision arrangements stressing elaborate understatement —behind the beat, as it were—and no holds barred as to instrumentation (French horns, tubas, harpsichords, and squads of violins are not uncommon). A feature of this style is its sophisticatedly vertical (chordal) and linear (contrapuntal) treatment, which is to say an over-all prevalence of standard "longhair" techniques in crew-cut disguise. Hence the deadly serious interest of those young intellectuals whose fathers scorned swing as unworthy of auditory attention.

Ever more varied punctuation being of the essence in this articulate dialect that is trying so hard to become a language, the "new sounds" of progressive jazz have unashamedly included (in the semantic subdivision of "Afro-Cuban") even the humble bongo drums and other implements of primitive cultures where no self-respecting musician would think of proceeding from tonic to dominant via a progression of minor sevenths.

If ragtime, jazz, swing, bebop, and "progressive" jazz had remained solely in the province of Broadway and of the dance and entertainment field, we should not be concerned with them in this volume. They have, however, exerted such a profound effect on art music, particularly with their rhythmic patterns, that they are one of the most important factors in modern music. This may be because jazz is so thoroughly expressive and characteristic of many features of our twentieth-century life; of the restlessness, the overturning of tradition, the economic, social, and political upheavals of the last few decades. In fact, it was so much an expression of the 1920's that those years are known to us, and will probably go down in history, as the "jazz age." Added to all this is the emotional fury of the two most devastating wars that have ever been inflicted on mankind. Why shouldn't the music of such times be dislocated and out of step?

It is not only in America that serious composers have incorporated jazz ideas into their works. American dance music has always been popular abroad, particularly in Paris; so even before American symphonists had begun to experiment with native jazz, such composers as Stravinsky with his *Ragtime*, Milhaud with his *La Création du monde*, Tansman with his *Triptych*, Křenek with *Jonny spielt auf*, and dozens of others were making capital of these typically American pat-

terns. Whether or not they succeeded in producing the real
thing, or only a synthetic imitation, is a matter for debate.

In America, of course, there have been dozens, if not
hundreds, of composers who have dipped into the jazz grab
bag for native material. John Alden Carpenter incorporated
jazz patterns in his ballets, *Skyscrapers* and *Krazy Kat*. Louis
Gruenberg, born in Russia in 1884 but living in America
since he was two years old, made sincere attempts to over-
come the rigidity of jazz in *Jazettes, The Daniel Jazz, The
Creation,* and a Jazz Suite for Orchestra. Edward Burlingame
Hill (1872) made a gentlemanly bow to jazz in his Jazz
Studies for Two Pianos, and we have already learned how
Aaron Copland turned to jazz in his early works and then
decided he had had enough of it, because its expressive pos-
sibilities were too limited.

The fact that jazz is primarily a dance vehicle and that it
is based on a regular, monotonous, four-beat foundation are
in themselves serious limitations. If the composer does away
with the fixed background, he ceases to write jazz. It is quite
true that jazz has elements that are unmistakably American, and indisputably twentieth-century, and there can be
no doubt that the impression it has made will be a lasting
one, for it has introduced elements in music that will be
useful to composers for many generations. It is not so certain,
however, that in its native, primal state it has proved fully
satisfying and rewarding to composers of art music.

The composers already cited have been musicians who
approached the popular medium of jazz from the viewpoint
of the concert hall and grand opera house. They are musicians who have been educated in the conservatories or by
private teachers steeped in the traditions of so-called serious
music, and they have turned to jazz in the same way that
art composers for many generations have drawn upon the
folk music of the people.

There is, however, another group that has approached the matter from the opposite direction. These composers have started their careers as Tin-Pan Alley song writers, and have graduated, if that is the word, to the regions of the concert hall. Generally they have produced a more genuine jazz product than those who started from the concert hall, but have been handicapped by lack of symphonic technique.

The best-known member of this group is the late George Gershwin (1898–1937) who started his musical career as a song plugger for a Broadway publishing firm. He soon began writing songs of his own, chiefly for musical comedies, which were so spontaneous, so gay and fresh in their unexpected twists of rhythm, melody, and harmony, that their composer was soon looked upon as one of our most promising Broadway talents. In 1924 the greater Gershwin emerged and startled the music world with a symphonic work for piano and orchestra that incorporated all the instrumental, harmonic, and rhythmic elements of jazz: his *Rhapsody in Blue,* played for the first time at Paul Whiteman's historic concert of symphonic jazz. From that time Gershwin played a dual role; he enjoyed a flourishing Broadway career that was extended to Hollywood, and also composed a succession of serious works that have become standard items in the symphonic repertoire: the Concerto in F, for piano and orchestra; *An American in Paris;* a Second Rhapsody; a set of Preludes for Piano (which have been scored for orchestra), and the Negro folk opera, *Porgy and Bess,* produced by the Theatre Guild in 1935, and revived for a record-breaking run on Broadway in the forties and for a world tour in the fifties.

Whatever may be said of Gershwin, one thing is certain: he produced a jazz product that was the real thing, a Broadway treatment of the Negro folk idiom. He did not turn out the polite jazz that serious composers who adopted it consciously have been accustomed to write. Gershwin's scores

are racy and native, and self-conscious only in their attempt
to be something more than they really are. He had his limitations and was sometimes at a loss to cover a large canvas
consistently and with coherent unity; but in everything he
wrote he kept the tunefulness, the gayety and sparkle, that
rendered all his works spontaneous and real.

There are others who have started on Broadway or with
dance bands, as composers or arrangers. Ferde Grofé
(1892——), composer of the *Grand Canyon Suite*, *Three
Shades of Blue*, *Mississippi Suite*, and other works, was arranger for Paul Whiteman, and it was he who orchestrated
Gershwin's *Rhapsody in Blue*. Robert Russell Bennett
(1894——), composer of the opera *Maria Malibran* and
a number of symphonic pieces, is a skilled arranger of scores
for musical comedies. William Grant Still (1895——), the
Negro composer of an *Afro-American Symphony*, and of
works that enjoy frequent performances by symphony orchestras, learned his trade by arranging and orchestrating for
W. C. Handy, Paul Whiteman, and Don Voorhees.

Recognition of jazz as a genuine musical expression has
accomplished two results: it has provided serious composers
with an idiom, however limited, which has brought freshness and a new spirit into their work. It has also raised to
the level of serious composers a number of genuinely creative
musicians from the popular field who have had something
original to say in a manner that is true to twentieth-century
American life.

Parenthetically, it should be noted that a few composers
have preferred to write directly within the jazz milieu—not
borrowing from it for a stylized "serious" piece but, if anything, bringing the stylizations of serious form into the dance
hall as it were (except that *aficionados* insist on intent listening and eschew dancing altogether). We are referring to
composers like Teo Macero, Will Hudson, Rayburn Wright,

Kenyon Hopkins, and Lyle Murphy. Their works are called jazz, but unlike earlier specimens they are fully written out, not improvisatory. By definition, then, they are not really jazz, for no old-time Dixieland man would stand for anything that has to be read, sometimes even conducted, if you please, to avoid chaos. Anyone's definition of jazz is a subjective proposition, however. Perhaps, as "Fats" Waller once said: "If you gotta ask what it is, you'll never know."

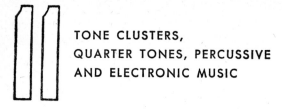

TONE CLUSTERS,
QUARTER TONES, PERCUSSIVE
AND ELECTRONIC MUSIC

A NUMBER OF YEARS AGO A YOUNG MAN NAMED HENRY COWELL brought a letter of introduction to a manufacturer of player pianos and records. It seemed that he was a pianist-composer who had some new ideas about piano-playing. He was invited to give a demonstration. Instead of using his fingers on the keys, he went to work with the palms of his hands, and finally with his entire forearms, striking whole blocks of keys at once.

The astonished merchants were aware that Cowell had already made something of a stir in the music world, and that he was being taken seriously in some quarters. They decided it might be a good idea to have him make a recording.

Several months later Cowell realized that he had not heard the record of his own playing, so he dropped in at the nearest store where this particular brand of records was sold. Without telling who he was, he asked to hear his piece. The clerk found it on the shelves, and inserted it in one of the pianos near the door. As the piano started to play, all the keys on the left side of the keyboard went down. In the next instant those of the right side went down. The clerk rushed to the piano. "Maybe this one is working," he said, as he took the roll out of the first piano and put it in another. The same performance was repeated, and the clerk began to perspire. "Our service man checks these pianos early in the morning," he said: "I guess he was out late last night." Being something of a wag, Cowell let the panicky clerk try a third piano, and then enlightened him.

Since then Henry Cowell (1897——) has become one of the leaders of American modernists in the experimental field, and has been regarded in some quarters as the inventor of the so-called tone clusters, or the striking, or sounding, of whole blocks, or groups, of tones simultaneously. He is not the first to employ tone clusters; Leo Ornstein used them a quarter-century ago, and Charles Ives has written chords that must be played with a board or a ruler. Cowell, however, has gone about their development more scientifically than his predecessors, and has devised a logical basis and explanation for their use.

When Ornstein introduced them, he called them "note clusters." At that time he was the leading radical among American composers. Some conservative critics felt that he was going in for the bizarre and startling merely because his early, conventional compositions had failed to attract much attention. To correct this state of affairs, they said, he shocked his audiences with such works as his *Wild Men's Dance,* in which he flung notes together on paper so closely that engravers had to invent new stems at crazy angles to show what notes should be struck together.

Ornstein was born in Russia in 1895 and has lived in America since 1907. He made his debut as a concert pianist in 1911, and was recognized as a musician of superior gifts. As a composer, he first produced some pieces that were altogether in traditional style, and were for the most part innocuous and undistinguished. Then, suddenly, he burst forth as a revolutionary who had thrown aside all pretense of convention. The change is described by Frederick H. Martens:

". . . He found himself, after he had written much music in the major-minor system, employing traditional forms, at a serious loss to express in music those deeper and more

intimate emotions and reactions within him which clamored
for utterance. And then, after unhappy weeks of hopeless-
ness and disorientation, of groping and experiment, it came
to him with overwhelming suddenness—that he had dis-
covered the alphabet of a new tongue, a tonal language
which enabled him to give his inspiration the freest rein in
sound expression." [1]

These sentences were written in 1918, when some of Arnold
Schoenberg's new pieces were becoming known, but before
the prophet of atonality had brought his system to its final
completion in formulas and rules. Even at that early date,
however, Schoenberg was recognized as a scientist as well
as musician, and in comparing Ornstein to Schoenberg,
Martens emphasized the fact that where Schoenberg was
mathematical, Ornstein was guided principally by his emotions.

In one paragraph, the author makes a direct comparison
between Schoenberg and Ornstein:

"The Wild Men's Dance, À la Chinoise, and the *Dwarf
Suite* . . . are the reflection of a logic of emotion—if one
may so call it—rather than of mathematical design. Here
we have the direct antithesis of Schoenberg, between whom
and Ornstein it is possible to draw some analogies—Ornstein's harmonies are the natural and unalloyed result of his
unfettered creative impulse, innocent of any preconceived
theory; Schoenberg, on the other hand, works in accord with
an abstruse and mysterious musical calculus known only
to himself. For Ornstein there exist no actual chords or discords. His chord combinations are not the conscious reflexion
of a definite theoretic basis, but the outcome of the impulse

[1] *Leo Ornstein, The Man—His Ideas—His Work.* New York: Breitkopf &
Haertel, 1918.

for a richer, fuller tonal coloring, one which extends the possibilities of pure harmony far beyond the limits of the diatonic system." [2]

Reflections on Ornstein's sincerity were probably unjust; he was a youngster who knew the rules, but who decided to throw them out the window and write to please himself.

He did attempt a partial explanation of his note clusters. They represented, he claimed, a "perfectly logical anticipation of overtones." This anticipation of overtones, by actual playing, enabled him to secure a certain depth of tone and an effect of "clouded sonority" that it was impossible to realize in any other way.[3] There is no further explanation of the relation between Ornstein's note clusters and overtones, but it is interesting to learn that the scientific and mathematical Henry Cowell bases his elaborate system of tone clusters on overtones, and arrives at somewhat the same effect, though more elaborately, through use of acoustic principles and calculation of sound vibrations.

Cowell was born in California. He was largely self-educated, and having an acquisitive mind and a keen intellect, he made a thorough job of teaching himself. When he made the acquaintance of an old upright piano, he tried all sorts of experiments upon it. He struck the keys, and he plucked the strings. When he turned himself loose on a grand piano, he studied the sounding board, and learned where it vibrated the most.

Delighted with the startling results he achieved from haphazard experiment, Cowell set out to justify his conclusions by becoming a scientist and making himself an authority on acoustics. In a chapter on Cowell in *American Composers on American Music* [4] Nicholas Slonimsky writes:

[2] *Ibid.*, pp. 41–42.   [3] *Ibid.*, p. 45.
[4] Stanford University Press; copyright 1933 by the Board of Trustees of Leland Stanford Junior University.

"It is rare to find a crusader in a big cause whose intellect is as strong as his battle-ax. Not all crusaders are more interested in their cause than themselves. Few are creators of original work in a field of art. Henry Cowell is the exceptional type who possesses all of these qualities. In Pushkin's fantastic tale of Mozart and Salieri, there are these amazing lines:

> And I dissected music as a corpse,
> By algebra I tested harmony of sounds, . . .

This scientific procedure Henry Cowell unashamedly resumes. If there is one rule in his creative art, it consists in taking nothing for granted. Harmony, rhythm, tone-color—Henry Cowell submits them to a test as though they were mere human beliefs, not laws."

In 1919 Cowell gathered his theories and ideas into a book, *New Musical Resources,* which was published in revised form eleven years later, in 1930. In the section on "Tone Combinations" he explains the underlying principle of his tone clusters. Showing how each musical tone, in its vibrations, produces overtones that follow a definite harmonic pattern, he then explains that each of the overtones produces its own subovertones. Thus, when the tone of C produces its primary overtones of G and E, the overtone G produces its subovertones of D and B; and overtone E its subovertones of B and G sharp. When the overtones of the original C are extended further to the higher harmonics, the multiplication continues, and includes every tone of the scale. The ear, according to Cowell's theory, hears these overtones when the tone of C is sounded alone, therefore the composer is merely following scientific laws when he has them sounded simultaneously. This theory obviously ignores the fact that when a single tone is sounded, the overtones are subsidiary in sound volume to the principal tone.

Another theory of tone clusters results from Cowell's method of constructing chords. Just as traditional harmony builds chords on intervals of the third, and the atonalists on fourths, Cowell suggests that they be built on seconds, or by tones that are nearest to each other in the scale. This, of course, produces tone clusters.

Cowell has also experimented widely and thoroughly in rhythms, particularly in polyrhythms, which are humanly impossible for a single player, or even groups of players, to perform. These rhythms have been devised according to the rate of vibration of the pitch of each tone. For the performance of these multiple and polyrhythms, mechanical instruments may be used—player pianos, or the Rhythmicon, an instrument Cowell developed in collaboration with Professor Leon Theremin, inventor of the ether-wave instrument that bears his name.

As a composer, Cowell writes in any number of styles, but basically in two: one embodies the scientific approach, and the other discloses his Celtic love for the weird, the colorful, the whimsical, and even the sentimental. In recent years his music has known considerable acceptance in the open market, and deservedly so, for few composers package so much expression so attractively. Among his more popular works are the *Hymn and Fuguing Tune* series (Nos. 2, 3, and 5 in particular), and the Fourth, Fifth, Tenth, and Eleventh of his symphonies—the last-named having been one of the more successful "Louisville Commissions" subsidized by the Rockefeller Foundation through the Louisville Orchestra.

Some composers have felt that with the introduction of atonality the possibilities of the present musical scale are exhausted, and that music can go no further toward new tonal combinations unless further tones are added. This, they say,

is possible only by dividing the half tone into smaller intervals. Thus, the term quarter tone has been introduced into
the music vocabulary to indicate the division of the half tone
into two quarter tones, so that the octave will consist of
twenty-four, instead of twelve, tones. Experiments have also
been made with still smaller intervals: the third tone, sixth
tone, eighth tone; and even the sixteenth tone.

Orientals have long used these smaller intervals. That is
why much of their music sounds out of tune to Western ears.
Until recently it was generally assumed that since Oriental
ears were untrained musically, according to Western standards, the Hindus and Arabs were unable to sing in tune.
Scientific study, however, has shown that these people invariably sing their music in the same manner, with the same
intervals, during constant repetition. They actually use these
intervals intentionally.

Among cultivated musicians, Ferruccio Busoni (1866–
1924) was a pioneer in using smaller intervals. Busoni was
an Italian composer, pianist, and teacher, and in his book,
A New Esthetic of Music, he showed how the possibilities
of the traditional scale could be exhausted. He suggested
that one-third tones be used, dividing the whole tone into
three steps instead of two.

Busoni was considerably ahead of his time, and his ideas
were mostly dreams for the future: of a piano that would
be built for tuning in smaller intervals, and of works written
in his "triparte" scale. Later composers have been able to
hear their ideas carried out, and to write quarter-tone music
which has been played, either on stringed instruments that
can produce tones at any pitch the player wishes, violin,
viola, 'cello, etc., or on especially constructed keyboard and
wind instruments.

Alois Hába, a Czechoslovakian composer born in 1893, is
among the most prominent of those who have written quarter-

tone music. The bulk of his early works were in the traditional half-tone system, but he has written many quartertone compositions: two operas—*The Mother* (1929) and *The Unemployed* (1932); three string quartets; violin and 'cello solo pieces; works for orchestra; and five suites and ten fantasies for piano. More recently he has been composing in sixth and twelfth tones.

Notation of quarter-tone music presents problems. Some composers indicate smaller intervals by notes of different shapes, and others draw lines through the stems of the notes, the direction of the lines showing whether the quarter tones lie above or below the half tones that the notes indicate in traditional music notation. Notation of still smaller intervals becomes even more complicated.

Julián Carrillo, a Mexican composer, born in 1875, has spent most of his life in research and experiment among small intervals of the scale. He has invented special instruments that can play these intervals: a quarter-tone guitar, an eighth-tone *octarina*, a French horn that plays sixteenth tones, and a sixteenth-tone *arpacitera*. Some of Carrillo's works once were recorded for the phonograph, notably his *Preludio a Cristóbal Colón*,[5] played in quarter, eighth, and sixteenth tones, by "The Thirteenth Sound Ensemble of Havana," an organization that uses Carrillo's new instruments. The sounds produced by this record are indeed novel and strange to unaccustomed ears. The opening notes of the guitar sound very much as though the performer were tuning his instrument before actually playing, and later passages closely resemble an air-raid siren. When a human voice enters the scene, one wonders how the singer is able to maintain the pitch. The whole affair reminds one of the story of the Chinese who was taken to his first symphony concert. He arrived early, before the orchestra had settled itself on the

[5] Columbia 7357-M; 78 rpm; withdrawn.

stage and gone through the tuning-up process. When asked afterward how he enjoyed the concert, he said that he liked best the part that came before the works on the printed program.

Nevertheless, there is a strange beauty in this Carrillo *Preludio*. It is weird and somewhat disconcerting, but it cannot by any means be dismissed as nonsense.

Among those who have developed systems of notation for small intervals are Nicholas Oboukhov (1892–1954) and the Russian émigré Ivan Vishnegradsky. Vishnegradsky has written quarter-tone music for strings, and for a quarter-tone piano made for him in Germany.

In America, one of the exponents of quarter-tone music was Hans Barth (1897–1956), a pianist who was born in Germany and was brought to this country as a child. Barth had constructed a piano with two keyboards and two sets of strings. The two sets of strings are tuned a quarter tone apart. In addition to a number of other works, he composed a quarter-tone Concerto for Piano and Strings, once performed by the Philadelphia Orchestra under Leopold Stokowski. It has not been repeated.

The eminent musicologist, Joseph Yasser (1893———), believes that where our present tonal system consists of twelve tones, seven of them primary and five auxiliary, the tonal system of the future should divide the octave into nineteen equal intervals with twelve primary and seven auxiliary tones. This, of course, would require an entirely new division of the octave, and could not utilize the present twelve-tone system by subdivision of the whole or half tone. Another musicologist, Arthur Fickenscher (1871–1954), divided the octave into sixty intervals, and designed an instrument, the "Polytone," to further his research.

Edgar Varèse, born in Paris in 1885, and living in America since the first World War, has not gone in for tone clusters or quarter tones as such, but since he uses percussion instruments extensively, sometimes eliminating all instruments that produce a definite pitch, he may properly be discussed in this chapter.

Once when Varèse was asked if he should be classified with this or that group of modernists, he replied: "Right wing, liberal, left wing, applied to any Art, what nonsense! I try to fly on my own wings."

In this he has certainly succeeded; no one will deny his originality. Lawrence Gilman once wrote: "The music of Edgar Varèse is the pure milk of Modernism. Mr. Varèse makes no such disgraceful compromise with euphony as do his more conventional brethren. Hearing Schoenberg's *Five Pieces* for orchestra, you will remember that Wagner once lived; hearing Casella's *Alta Notte* you will remember that Schoenberg still lives. Hearing Varèse's *Hyperprism* you remember only Varèse." [6]

Hyperprism, written in the 1920's, employs a chamber orchestra and a veritable host of the percussion instruments of which Varèse is so fond, in this case with an added set of sleighbells and a siren. Another piece, *Ionisation* (1931) is scored for sixteen instruments of "percussion, friction, and sibilation," the latter consisting of two sirens.

Criticism of Varèse has run all the way from his being called the greatest of modern American composers, and the author of sincere music of "remote and alien beauty," to condemnation of his works as "strong, arrogant, infinitely repellent." For himself, he denies the charge of seeking primarily for originality, he claims that he is not interested in novelty or virtuosity, but only in expressiveness.

The American John J. Becker (1886——) is another musician who is seeking for new orchestral sounds, not only through percussion instruments but with these in combina-

[6] New York *Herald Tribune*, December 17, 1924.

tion with the other resources of the orchestra. Thus he explains that certain instrumental combinations will produce an effect like the cutting of steel. His opinion of tradition is expressed in his own words: "Laws are made for imitators; creators make their own laws."

Becker has explored the possibilities of percussion instruments in his dance work *Obongo,* which is scored for twenty-nine of them. Others of his works include various so-called *Soundpieces,* some for string quartet, one a Piano Sonata; numerous orchestral works; and music for the church written in the style of Palestrina with highly dissonant counterpoint.

No discussion involving smaller scale-intervals would be nearly complete without at least a passing reference to the researches of Harry Partch, that staunch enemy of all orthodoxy who has not only devised a 43-tone scale but also contrived special instruments to play it and then gone on to compose music for it. In 1949 he set forth his theories as evolved up to then in a book entitled *Genesis of a Music,* published by the University of Wisconsin Press. No musical freethinker should deprive himself of this amazing (and eventually quite technical) volume. In lieu of that, much of Partch's music is available on (noncommercial) recordings.

Inevitably, a careful perusal of the tonal system would lead us to exotic lands, and we would soon discover that the musics of the world differ one from another mostly in the matter of rhythm, scales being rather more relative and convertible. It would be pointless for us to pursue this very far from the general listener's frame of reference, although infinite treasures await the curious in the already vast catalogues of folk music on recordings. Our emphasis must be on those domestically familiar composers who have made the exotic musics their own to one extent or another. Of these the most frequently encountered in the concert halls, and also well represented on recordings, are Alan Hohvaness

(Somerville, Mass., 1911), Peggy Glanville-Hicks (Melbourne 1912), Paul Bowles (New York City, 1911), Colin McPhee (Montreal, 1901), and the sometime atonalist Lou Harrison, mentioned earlier.

And finally, we must speak of the tape recorder, that electronic magic carpet that is expected to take us to new horizons of musical experience. Not even the "prepared" pianos and assorted other gimmicks of John Cage (Los Angeles, 1912) had equipped professionals or laymen to cope with these utterly new dimensions. Two of our leading educators, Otto Luening (Milwaukee, 1900) and Vladimir Ussachevsky (China, 1911) of Columbia University, joined forces to master the machine upon its appearance a few years ago. Individually and in tandem, they have become the principal composers for, and advocates of, this most flexibly expressive in theory of all musical media.

Ussachevsky writes apropos of his *Sonic Contours:* "In magnetic tape we have, for the first time, I believe, the multiple means of modifying musical sounds after they have been recorded, or while they are being recorded. This is possible because of the flexibility with which tape can be cut up, spliced in any order, reversed for playing backward, speeded up, or slowed down or erased at any point, and so on. . . . My own experiments up to this time have been restricted to the use of sounds well below and well above the conventional piano range; to modification of the tone quality of the sounds within conventional range; and to electronic repetition of any such sounds by means of a specially designed gadget. The sounds produced by the latter create a peculiarly dimensional effect, and permit many individual variations in dynamic level, in notes sounding simultaneously . . ."

Of all this one New York writer observed: "The strangest music this side of paranoia. . . . It employs a human voice (well, something human), a flute, piano, ship's horn, triangle, and certain reverberations of the magnetic tape. Bebop is old hat compared with this music. Schoenberg never had it so good and wild." That will give you the general idea.

However, what we have just quoted was from a feature story. Listen to a responsible critic, William Mootz of the Louisville *Courier-Journal,* on the *Rhapsodic Variations for Tape Recorder and Orchestra* by Luening and Ussachevsky: ". . . the composers have re-evaluated their conception of orchestral balances. The strings are used primarily to form a base of sound above which the woodwinds and brass carry independent material. Around and above all this, the tape recorder envelops the music in waves of unorthodox sound. The composers have electronically distorted and mixed their original sound track to arrive at different orchestral colors in much the same way a painter mixes his colors on a palette. The initial impact of the work gives one the impression of opposing and merging strata of sound, ingeniously conceived and worked out with striking rhythmic pliability.

"A basic weakness of the work, however, is that the hearer cannot help identifying some of the emanations from the speaker with more mundane associations. You hear roars from an air terminal, background effects from a cheap radio thriller, the staccato click of rolling dice, screeching brakes, or the unpleasant vibrato of an electronic organ. . . . What value does such a work have as music? Your guess is as good as mine. . . . One thing I do know. Luening and Ussachevsky cannot be dismissed as playboy pranksters. Too many men, not only in this country but also on the Continent, are following their same line of thought."

Add to this, in reflecting on such music, the following excerpts from a column by Paul Henry Lang in the New York *Herald Tribune* at the close of the 1955–56 season:

"I see by the papers that a new composition by John Cage, for ten solo radios, is to be performed, and I wonder whether a reckoning with the campaign to take away the creative process from the composer and give it to the machine is not overdue. . . .

"In a book entitled *Musical Engineering* (Prentice-Hall), Dr. Harry F. Olson, director of RCA Acoustical Laboratories, a distinguished physicist, goes on record as condemning all 'conventional' musical instruments (that's old Stradivari) as being primitive and outmoded. According to him only electronic instruments deserve to be considered in our modern age. This is only one of the many instances of the present trend in which the engineer assumes the role of arbiter of the arts.

"At that, we may be indulgent toward the scientist. He is carried away by his technological miracles, and in his zeal reaches out into territories that are not within his competence. What is deplorable is that he has been joined by musicians. . . .

"It is entirely legitimate and desirable to search for new sounds, and some remarkable developments have taken place in the last few years—the novel use of percussion instruments is a case in point. But to experiment in order to enrich music is one thing; it is quite another to substitute for works of art experiments which by their nature are lacking in musical organization in the artistic and human sense. The very moment when the active functioning of the creative mind is supplanted by happenings beyond its control we are no longer within the domain of art.

"I am glad to report that the American representatives of 'Musique concrète' frankly state that what they are doing is experimentation with a view to possible further use for *musical composition.* Whether they will succeed remains to be seen, but in the meantime let us play the piano as Mr. Steinway made it, blow into the front end of the clarinet, run the tape recorder at its normal speed and just compose music as it was conceived by the human brain; it is a difficult enough task . . ."

12
THE
COMPOSER AND
THE PUBLIC

THE COMPOSER'S IDIOM MAY NOT BE DIRECTLY RELATED TO THE conditions under which he works, but his existence as a composer is undoubtedly dependent on his status in the community. There is no greater fallacy than the time-honored tradition that composers and artists work best in garrets, or that the joy of creation, like virtue, is its own reward. The composer is nurtured by success and encouragement just as plants are nourished by fertile soil. There will always, we hope, be dedicated men like Charles Ives who keep on composing with no thought of whether their music will ever be heard, but the average composer is human enough to expect an audience for the music he writes, just as the automobile manufacturer makes cars for people to drive and not for dead storage.

Superficially it appears that the field of music is burdened with overproduction. Hundreds of really significant composers, in the United States and abroad, are producing many more works than the average music lover can ever hope to absorb. The result of this surplus is that the modern composer meets strong competition and many talented musicians are by necessity overlooked and neglected. Orchestras can play just so many new works each season, and they will always have their subscribers to consider when they introduce experimental music that is ahead of its time. Public resistance to the unfamiliar is still a strong deterrent to the programing of new music. The composer who has not yet received the approval of the larger music-loving public must still look to the "composers' forums" and other forward-looking, noncommercial groups to perform his works.

Yet, the mere fact that there are today composers producing far more music than the public will ever hear is in itself an indication that conditions have been favorable to the development and growth of contemporary music. Conditions in the United States alone show how far the composer has really advanced in this century. In the early 1900's American music was interesting chiefly to those who wrote it and to a few chauvinists who were determined that native music should have a chance to be heard. Composers were relatively few in number, at least those whose works were played with any frequency by the half-dozen important orchestras of the country. Now, in mid-century, American music is taken for granted and we number our composers by the hundreds rather than by dozens. In addition there are resident in America many of the leading twentieth-century composers from Europe, many of whom have become citizens, among them Stravinsky and the late Arnold Schoenberg.

The basic reason for this growth is that the composers are men of talent and have something interesting to say to us, but it is also apparent that the expanding market for which they produce their music has been an essential factor in their development. Moreover, the methods of disseminating music to the public have undergone revolutionary changes.

A prime factor, particularly in the United States, is the increased number of performing organizations. Rather than the half-dozen major orchestras at the turn of the century, there are now at least thirty high-budgeted symphony societies in the large cities and several hundred secondary groups playing regularly in smaller towns. Government statistics show that the people of this country spend more money on concerts and opera than they spend on baseball.

Radio and television bring music to people who cannot regularly attend live concerts, and phonograph records enable them to hear any kind of music they wish whenever they want to hear it. In fact, the development of long-playing records and high fidelity has probably done more to advance the musical taste of the public than any other medium. As recently as the 1920's and 1930's it was possible to hear modern, and particularly experimental, music only in the large cities where either a venturesome Stokowski or some intrepid group of pioneers would offer works too shocking for the conventionally conditioned ears of the general public. Owners of phonographs could buy records only of standard works, and the 78-rpm albums of major works were cumbersome.

LP records have changed all that. An hour-long work occupies only one record, and the available repertoire includes every type of music imaginable, from Palestrina to Varèse. Instead of being conservative and timid about issuing records of untried and unfamiliar music the manufacturers are often more venturesome than the average conductor of a symphony orchestra. A glance at the record list at the end of this volume will show that anyone who wants to be familiar with even the most experimental of our contemporary composers may listen at home to specimens of their work. In addition to their use in homes records are available to radio stations who broadcast them repeatedly. In the large centers such stations as New York's WQXR and WNYC play records of contemporary music in almost equal ratio to those of the standard repertory.

This has brought about a revolutionary change in the dissemination of music. An Ives or a John Cage can find an immediate audience. Formerly a work had to be established in the concert repertoire before it was recorded, whereas today it is often made available on records before the audiences for live concerts have had a chance to hear it. This has not only provided an immediate audience for the composer; it has also helped to increase his income. And the composer's economic welfare is important, for if we are to have composers, they, like any workmen, must eat.

Early in the century it was impossible for anyone in this country to make a living merely by composing. Even Mac-Dowell had to turn to concertizing and teaching. The composer not only received small return from his major compositions, he generally had to provide at his own effort and expense manuscript scores and parts to any orchestras willing to play them. Conditions are still far from the millennium in this regard, but there are agencies and positions that enable a composer to devote his major efforts to composing.

A number of universities offer composer-in-residence positions where the incumbent's principal job is not to teach, but to compose. There are also fellowships and grants, and an increasing number of prize contests that may or may not (too often the latter) produce significant results. More satisfactory than prize contests are commissions of new works from composers by various organizations, by symphony orchestras, and in many cases by individuals. The late Serge Koussevitzky was a great leader in this direction during the years he led the Boston Symphony, and today the Koussevitzky Foundation is continuing this encouragement to contemporary composers. The Louisville Symphony Orchestra, through funds from the Rockefeller Foundation, commissions each year a large number of new works and guarantees to perform them and to record them.

The primary use of music is its performance. Publication

is only a convenient means of making performance possible. Publication of books is an end in itself. Those who buy them read them, but the printing of concert music is only providing a script or scenario to those who will bring it to life by performing it in public. It is therefore logical that the composer should derive his livelihood directly from the primary use of his product—its performance.

The copyright laws of most countries give to the owner of a copyrighted musical work (either the composer himself or his assignee) the exclusive right to perform that work in public. In the United States this right is limited to public performance *for profit*. In France and the British Commonwealth and in most foreign countries anyone who performs copyrighted music in public, even in schools and churches, must have a license to do so. In America the composer cannot collect unless it can be established that the performer or the entrepreneur is profiting from the performance. Consequently the "for profit" limitation has caused much argument and even litigation to determine what performances are given for profit and which are exempt. When radio first came into being the broadcasters maintained that inasmuch as the audience itself did not pay for the programs they were not for profit. Court decisions were required to establish the principle that broadcasting was a profit-making enterprise.

Assertion of the performing right would be an impossible task for the individual composer, and securing a license to perform would be equally difficult, if the users had to seek out the copyright owner of each piece they wish to perform. For this reason there are in almost every country "performing rights" societies that administer these rights for composers and publishers by licensing the users of music and distributing the moneys received among their members (the composers and publishers) according to the number of performances each has received. Most of the societies are known by their initials: in England, PRS (Performing Right Society, Limited); in France, SACEM (Société des Auteurs, Compositeurs et Editeurs de Musique); in Germany, GMA (Gesellschaft für Musikalische Aufführungs und Mechanische Vervielfältigungsrechte); and in the United States, ASCAP (American Society of Composers, Authors and Publishers) as well as BMI (Broadcast Music, Inc.), organized by the broadcasters themselves, and SESAC (Society of European Stage Authors and Composers), a privately owned corporation. The number of foreign societies with which ASCAP has reciprocal agreements is twenty-nine.

In America the justice of paying the composer for the right to use his music has not been easily gained. It is readily conceded that hall rent, lighting bills, printing of programs, janitors' salaries, piano tuning, are necessary expenses, but payment to the man who has composed the raw material without which there would be no concert has required much persuasion and in some cases court action. The "for profit" limitation of the copyright act prevents composers whose works are used chiefly by choral societies, schools, and churches from collecting any payment from such organizations for the performance of their music.

Nevertheless, the licensing of those users of music who are ostensibly operating for profit has enabled many composers whose works are regularly played by such agencies to derive a substantial income from the performance of their works.

So much for the atmosphere in which our composers work and the conditions that produce what they write and, indirectly, the kind and quality of the music they compose. We must always remember that these men and women are writing in our time, and to be a valid expression their music must reflect not Beethoven's age, but ours. The listener must become familiar with the fundamental differences between yesterday's music and that of today and learn to listen to atonal or polytonal music with a different set of standards from those he applies to the old masters. No one can expect the same kind of pleasure from Stravinsky's *Rite of Spring* that he receives from *The Swan* of Saint-Saëns, nor will he derive from a modern dance band the same experience he had from listening to the dance orchestra of yesterday playing the *Blue Danube*.

It is essential that we remember that today's modern music is *our* music, written in our time. Our age is not the age of our grandfathers, nor even of our fathers. Our music, therefore, reflects what has been going on about us, and if it fails to picture these things, it is dishonest and false.

The listener who approaches modern music must put aside the idea that it will give him the same emotional reactions he gets from Beethoven or Mendelssohn. From them he gets a response that is almost a direct reflex. His immediate reaction to modern music will be entirely different, and he will have to condition his natural reflex with an intellectual control that will enable him to look upon new music objectively, and decide what it is all about.

Consequently, a new yardstick must be adopted if the listener is to form a well-reasoned opinion of his own about the new music he hears. He must shelve for the moment the question of whether or not he likes it. He probably won't, but that does not mean that he will not come to like some of this music when he has heard it a few times.

First, he should decide whether the music is a true expression of the present day, or of the era in which it was written. It may, of course, represent any one, or several, of the multiple phases of our existence—idealism, unrest, optimism or pessimism, the will to freedom, hope, or despair. It may be music that comes from a free people, or from one that is in bondage.

If the listener becomes sufficiently acquainted with the architectural structure of music, so that he can follow instinctively the relation of various sections of a composition to the whole, then he can judge for himself whether the new work is coherent and unified, and whether or not the composer arrives at the place he set out for.

The listener can decide, too, whether the dissonances he hears serve an artistic purpose. They will probably disturb him; that is inevitable at first, but he can at least judge whether or not they are essential to the composer's purpose, and whether they are effective in achieving that end. When he hears polytonal music, and knows that it is employing combined keys, or tonalities, he can decide whether such a combination adds new colors to the composer's palette.

There will, of course, be an emotional reaction; maybe it will be violent. The listener must then judge whether his emotions are those the composer intended him to have. The new piece may fill him with anger, it may give him a sense of unrest or excitement, it may even soothe him, or it may exalt him. If it does anything except bore him, it has accomplished some purpose, and time is needed to decide whether that purpose is worthwhile.

It is wiser, however, to consider listening to new music an intellectual sport at first, for as such it can easily prove fascinating. Then, when the strange idioms are no longer strange, the emotional pleasure will come automatically. Tomorrow you will come to like the best of today's modern music.

It is perhaps idle to speculate on what the music of the future will be; whether it will go on developing new dissonances to confuse us: quarter tones and new scales that will always keep us a few steps behind the composers, and cause writers to keep on writing books on modern music. It is safe to prophesy, however, that the future condition of the human race will determine the course our music will take. If there is continued strife and unrest, music will be clashing and restless; if there is peace, it will reflect our composure as well as our complex civilization.

It is well to consider the qualities that have marked the enduring music of the past. Some of the most revolutionary works have lived the longest, but it is not likely that their revolutionary character, in itself, has been responsible for their immortality.

Carl Engel had some shrewd words to say on this subject a number of years ago, in an article from which we have already quoted:

"The general hysteria of the moment finds vent in grotesqueness, exaggeration and caricature. The tonal material, made subservient to these ends, has yielded astonishing offshoots and unsuspected fascinations. Yet here, too, surfeit will be reached sooner or later and change will be inevitable. Perhaps even, after the welter of mock-passion, a benign fate may lead mankind to re-discover serenity. For the noblest music, among admittedly great music, is that which fills the hearer with a serene earnestness and calm." [1]

The reaction against the extreme has already taken place. Certainly Arnold Schoenberg passed from the outermost realms of atonality to music that is far less bizarre, and that sounds rather conventional in comparison with his experimental works. Stravinsky, too, has softened his sharpest and hardest edges. One thing is certain, it is no longer fashionable to shock audiences just for the sake of startling them out of

[1] "Harking Back and Looking Forward," *Musical Quarterly*, January, 1928.

their complacency. Nobody is very smug these days, so it isn't as much fun to upset people.

It is probably true that the height of the early twentieth-century experimentation has been passed. A vast number of new styles and methods have been tried, and some of them have been kept and some discarded. We have probably come to the time when composers have sampled enough of the new systems to have found what has served their purpose, and what is useless to them. They have absorbed into their own techniques various of the new devices and have become accustomed to using them. And since they are no longer new toys, they have learned how to use them with discretion and taste. And as pure experimentation passes, true creativeness steps in, and art takes the place of science.

All of this may well usher in a new era of music, and bring to the middle of the twentieth century a golden age from which a new music will come, built upon the best of former centuries. It will make use of new materials, but it is safe to prophesy that it will be not the experiments that will in themselves survive, but rather their adoption and integration by composers capable of using them for expressive ends, not merely because they are new and startling.

SELECTED READING LIST

BAUER, MARION. *Twentieth Century Music,* rev. ed. G. P. Putnam's Sons, New York, 1947.

COPLAND, AARON. *Our New Music.* Whittlesey House, New York, 1941.

CORLE, EDWIN. *Igor Stravinsky.* Duell, Sloan & Pearce, Inc., New York, 1949.

COWELL, HENRY. *New Musical Resources.* Alfred A. Knopf, Inc., New York, 1930.

COWELL, HENRY AND SYDNEY H. *Charles Ives and His Music.* Oxford University Press, Inc., 1955.

COWELL, HENRY, editor. *American Composers on American Music: A Symposium.* Stanford University Press, Stanford, California, 1933.

EWEN, DAVID. *The Book of Modern Composers,* rev. ed. Alfred A. Knopf, Inc., New York, 1950.

EWEN, DAVID. *The Complete Book of 20th Century Music.* Prentice-Hall, Inc., New York, 1952.

GRAY, CECIL. *A Survey of Contemporary Music.* Oxford University Press, Inc., New York, 1927.

HELMHOLTZ, HERMANN VON. *Sensations of Tone.* Longmans, Green & Co., Inc., New York, 1912.

HEYMANN, KATHARINE, RUTH. *The Relation of Ultra-Modern to Archaic Music.* Small, Maynard & Company, Boston, 1921.

HOBSON, WILDER. *American Jazz Music.* W. W. Norton, 1939.

HOWARD, JOHN TASKER. *Our American Music,* rev. with supplementary chapters by James Lyons. Thomas Y. Crowell Company, New York, 1954.

HOWARD, JOHN TASKER. *Our Contemporary Composers.* Thomas Y. Crowell Company, New York, 1941.

KŘENEK, ERNST. *Music Here and Now.* W. W. Norton & Company, Inc., New York, 1939.

LEIBOWITZ, RENÉ. *Schoenberg and His School.* Philosophical Library, Inc., New York, 1949.

LENORNAUD, RENÉ. *Study of Modern Harmony.* Boston Music Co., Boston, 1915.

MAISEL, EDWARD M. *Charles T. Griffes; The Life of an American Composer.* Alfred A. Knopf, Inc., New York, 1943.

MILLER, DAYTON C. *Science of Musical Sounds.* The Macmillan Company, New York, 1916.

MILLER, HORACE ALDEN. *New Harmonic Devices.* Oliver Ditson Company, Inc., Philadelphia, 1930.

PANASSIE, HUGUES. *The Real Jazz.* Smith & Durrell, Inc., New York, 1942.

PANNAIN, GUIDO. *Modern Composers.* E. P. Dutton & Co., Inc., New York, 1933.

PLEASANTS, HENRY. *The Agony of Modern Music.* Simon and Schuster, Inc., New York, 1955.

REDFIELD, JOHN. *Music: A Science and an Art.* Alfred A. Knopf, Inc., New York, 1928.

SARGEANT, WINTHROP. *Jazz, Hot and Hybrid,* new and enl. ed. E. P. Dutton & Co., Inc., New York, 1946.

SLONIMSKY, NICOLAS. *Music Since 1900.* Coleman-Ross Company, Boston, 1949.

SMITH, JULIA. *Aaron Copland, His Work and Contribution to American Music.* E. P. Dutton & Co., Inc., New York, 1955.

STRAVINSKY, IGOR. *About My Life.* Simon and Schuster, Inc., New York, 1936.

TANSMAN, ALEXANDRE. *Igor Stravinsky. The Man and His Music.* G. P. Putnam's Sons, New York, 1949.

THOMPSON, OSCAR. *Debussy, Man and Artist.* Dodd, Mead & Co., New York, 1937.

SELECTED RECORDINGS

Orchestra code

ARSO	American Recording Society	CISO	Cincinnati
		CO	Cleveland Orchestra
BATO	Ballet Theatre	COA	Concertgebouw of Amsterdam
BBC	British Broadcasting Co.		
		CRSO	Cologne Radio Symphony
BEPO	Berlin Philharmonic	CSO	Chicago Symphony
BFO	Brazilian Festival		
		DASO	Dallas Symphony
BLSO	Baltimore Little Symphony	DNO	Danish National
BNO	Belgrade National Opera	DSO	Detroit Symphony
BOO	Barcelona Opera	DSRSO	Danish State Radio Symphony
BPO	Boston Pops		
BRO	Bavarian Radio Chorus	EOE	English Opera Ensemble
BSO	Boston Symphony	ERSO	Eastman-Rochester Symphony
BTO	Bolshoi Theatre		
CAO	Concert Arts	GSO	"Golden Symphony Orchestra"
CBSS	CBS Symphony		
CCO	Colonne Concert		
CETO	Champs-Elysées Théâtre	HO	Hallé (Manchester)

HP	Hamburg Phil-	ONSS	Orchestra of the
	harmonic		New Sym-
JSLA	Janssen Sym-		phony Soci-
	phony of Los		ety
	Angeles	OSR	Orchestre de la
KOA	Kentucky Opera		Suisse Ro-
	Association		mande
LAO	Lamoreux	PCO	Paris Conserva-
LEO	Leipzig Philhar-		tory
	monic	PHO	Philharmonia
LO	Louisville	PMS	Pro Musica
LPO	London Philhar-	PNTO	Prague National
	monic		Theatre
LPSO	"Philharmonic	PO	Philadelphia
	Symphony of	PPHO	Paris Philhar-
	London"		monic
LSO	London Sym-	PPO	Philharmonic
	phony		Promenade
MGM	M-G-M Orches-	PSO	Pittsburgh Sym-
	tra		phony
MMCO	Musical Master-	RCAVS	RCA Victor
	piece Society		Symphony
	Chamber Or-	RFO	Radiodiffusion
	chestra		Française
MOO	Metropolitan	RHDO	Robin Hood
	Opera		Dell
MSO	Minneapolis	RIASO	RIAS
	Symphony	RPO	Royal Philhar-
MUOO	Munich Opera		monic
MXSO	Mexico Sym-	RRSO	Radio Rome
	phony		Symphony
NASO	National Sym-	SCA	St. Cecilia Acad-
	phony (Wash-		emy
	ington, D. C.)	SFO	Stockholm Festi-
NBCSO	NBC Symphony		val
NSO	New Symphony	SFSO	San Francisco
NYCBO	New York City		Symphony
	Ballet	SLS	Saidenberg Lit-
NYP	Philharmonic-		tle Symphony
	Symphony of	SRO	State (USSR)
	New York		Radio

SRS(O)	Stockholm Radio Symphony (Orchestra)	ES	Esoteric
		HMV	His Master's Voice
		HS	Haydn Society
		I	Innovations
SSO	"Schuyler Symphony Orchestra"	KEN	Kendall
		L	London
		LOU	Louisville (subscription only; address Louisville Orchestra, 830 S. 4th St., Louisville 3, Ky.)
VO	Vienna		
VOO, VSOO	Vienna (State) Opera		
VOS	Vienna Orchestral Society	M	Mercury
VPO	Vienna Philharmonic	MGM	Metro-Goldwyn-Mayer
VSO	Vienna Symphony	ML	Music Library
		MMS	Musical Masterpiece Society (subscription only; address 71 Fifth Avenue, NYC 3)
ZS	Zimbler Sinfonietta		

Record label code

		NR	New Records
A	Angel	OV	Overtone
ARS	American Recording Society (subscription only; address ARS, 100 Sixth Ave., NYC 13)	P	Period
		PHIL	Philharmonia
		PO	Polymusic
		R	Remington
		SPA	Society of Participating Artists (usually SPA)
C	Columbia		
CA	Camden (RCA Victor)		
		STRAD	Stradivari
CAP	Capitol	U	Unicorn
CE	Classic Editions	UR	Urania
CHS	Concert Hall Society	V	RCA Victor
CRI	Composers Recordings	VG	Vanguard
		VOX	Vox
D	Decca	W	Westminster
EP	Epic (Columbia)		

ANTHEIL, George (b. Trenton, New Jersey, 1900)
Ballet mécanique; NY Percussion Group; (C) ML-4956
BADINGS, Henk (b. Bandoeng, Java, 1907)
The Louisville Symphony; Whitney, LO; LOU-56-6

BARBER, Samuel (b. West Chester, Pennsylvania, 1910)
  Adagio for Strings, Op. 11; Essay for Orchestra, Op. 12, No. 1;
    School for Scandal Overture; Hanson, ERSO; (M) MG-40002
  Capricorn Concerto, Op. 21 (for flute, trumpet, oboe); Baker, Frei-
    stadt, Miller, SLS; (CHS) CHS-1078
  Concerto for Cello and Orchestra; Nelsova, Barber, NSO; (L) LPS-
    332
  Dover Beach; Songs; Symphony No. 1; King, Quincy, Hartt Quartet;
    (CE) 1011
  Hermit Songs; Price, Barber; (C) ML-4988
  Quartet in D Major, Op. 11; Stradivari Quartet; (STRAD) 602
  Sonata for Cello and Piano, Op. 6; Piatigorsky, Berkowitz; (V) LM-
    2013
  Souvenirs, Op. 28; Gold & Fizdale; (C) ML-4855
  Symphony No. 2, Op. 19; Medea (ballet suite), Op. 23; Barber,
    NSO; (L) LL-1328
  Violin Concerto, Op. 14; Kaufman, Goehr, orchestra; (MMS) MMS-
    105
BARLOW, Wayne (b. Elyria, Ohio, 1912)
  The Winter's Past; Hanson, ERSO; (M) MG-40003
BARTÓK, Béla (b. Hungary, 1881; d. New York, 1945)
  Concerto for Orchestra; Ormandy, PO; (C) ML-4973
  Music for Strings, Percussion and Celesta; Dance Suite; Fricsay,
    RIASO; (D) DL-9747
  Piano Music; Foldes; (D) DL-9801/4
  Sonata for Violin Unaccompanied; Contrasts for Violin, Clarinet, and
    Piano; Mann, Drucker, Hambro; (Bartók) 916
  String Quartets I–VI; Juilliard Quartet; (C) ML-4278/80
BAUER, Marion (b. Walla Walla, Washington, 1887)
  Suite for Strings; Prelude and Fugue; Adler, VO; CRI 101
BAX, Sir Arnold Edward Trevor (b. London, 1883; d. Cork, 1953)
  Garden of Fand; Barbirolli, HO; (M) MG-50115
  Tintagel; Boult, LPO; (L) LL-1169
BERG, Alban (b. Vienna, 1885; d. Vienna, 1935)
  Violin Concerto; Krasner, Rodzinski, CO; (C) ML-4857
  Wozzeck; Soloists, Mitropoulos, NYP; (C) SL-118
BERGER, Arthur (b. New York, 1912)
  Duo for Cello and Piano; Quartet in C Major for Winds; Greenhouse,
    Makas, Fairfield ensemble; (C) ML-4846
  Serenade Concertante; Solomon, ensemble; (MGM) E-3245

BERGSMA, William (b. Oakland, California, 1921)
Wife of Martin Guerre (excerpts); Waldman, original cast; CRI-
105X
BERNSTEIN, Leonard (b. Lawrence, Massachusetts, 1918)
Age of Anxiety (Symphony No. 2); Foss, Bernstein, NYP; (C) ML-
4325
Fancy Free; Bernstein, orchestra; (C) CL-920
Jeremiah Symphony; Facsimile; Bernstein, SSO, GSO; (CA) CAL-
196
BLITZSTEIN, Marc (b. Philadelphia, 1905)
Excerpts from The Cradle Will Rock, No For An Answer, Regina;
Various artists, Blitzstein (narrator); (W) SA-717
BLOCH, Ernest (b. Switzerland, 1880)
Baal Shem; Violin Concerto; Szigeti, Munch, PCO; (C) ML-4679
Concerto Grosso (No. 1); Steinberg, PSO; (CAP) S-8212
String Quartets I–IV; Griller Quartet; (L) LLA-23
Schelomo; Voice in the Wilderness; Nelsova, Ansermet, LSO; (L)
LL-1232
BOWLES, Paul Frederic (b. New York, 1911)
Music for a Farce; Scènes d'Anabase; Various artists; (C) ML-4845
A Picnic Cantata; Gold & Fizdale; (C) ML-5068
BRANT, Henry Dreyfus (b. Montreal, Canada, 1913)
Signs and Alarms; Galaxy 2; Chamber ensemble; (C) ML-4956
BRITTEN, Benamin (b. England, 1913)
Diversions for piano and orchestra; Sinfonia da Requiem; Katchen,
Britten, LSO, DSRSO; (L) LL-1123
Les Illuminations; Serenade for Tenor, Horn and Strings; Pears,
Goossens, NSO; (L) LL-994
A Simple Symphony, Op. 4; Ceremony of Carols; Goossens, NSO;
(L) LL-1336
Young Persons' Guide to the Orchestra; Four Sea Interludes and
Pasacaglia from Peter Grimes; Van Beinum, COA; (L) LL-917
CAAMANO, Roberto (b. Buenos Aires, 1923)
Magnificat, Op. 20; Whitney, LO; LOU-56-3
CAGE, John (b. Seattle, 1913)
Quartet (1950); New Music Quartet; (C) ML-4495
CARPENTER, John Alden (b. Park Ridge, Illinois, 1876; d. Chicago,
1951)
Adventures in a Perambulator; Swoboda, VSOO; (CHS) CHS-1140
Skyscrapers; von Zallinger, ARSO; ARS-37

CARTER, Elliott (b. New York, 1908)
  The Minotaur (Ballet Suite); Hanson, ERSO; (M) MG-50103
  Sonata for Piano; Sonata for Violoncello & Piano; Webster, Greenhouse, Makas; (ARS) ARS-25
CHÁVEZ, Carlos (b. Mexico City, 1899)
  Corrido de "El Sol"; Sinfonia India; Obertura Republicana; Chávez, MXSO; (D) DL-9527
  La Hija de Colquide; Chávez, MXSO; (D) DL-7512
  Sonatina for Violin and Piano; A & M Ajemian; (MGM) E-3180
  Toccata for Percussion; Boston Percussion Group; (Boston) 207
CHOU Wen-chung (b. Chefoo, China, 1923)
  "And The Fallen Petals"; Whitney, LO; LOU-56-1
CLAFLIN, Avery (b. Keene, New Hampshire, 1898)
  Fishhouse Punch; Adler, VO; (CRI) CRI-107
COPLAND, Aaron (b. Brooklyn, 1900)
  Appalachian Spring; El Salón México; Koussevitzky, BSO; (V) LCT-1134
  Billy the Kid; Levine, BATO; (CAP) P-8238
  Piano Concerto, 1926; Smit, Copland, RRSO; (MMS) MMS-105
  Sonata for Piano; Bernstein; (CA) CAL-214
  Symphony No. 3 (1946); Dorati, MSO; (M) MG-50018
COWELL, Henry Dixon (b. Menlo Park, California, 1897)
  Hymn and Fuguing Tunes, Nos. 2 and 5; Adler, VOS; (U) 1011
  Selected Piano Works; Cowell; (CRI) CRI-109
  Symphony No. 4; Hanson, ERSO; (M) MG-40005
  Symphony No. 7; Strickland, VSO; (MGM) MGM-3084
  Symphony No. 10; Fiddler's Jig; Adler, VSO; (U) UNLP-1008
  Symphony No. 11; Whitney, LO; (C) KL-5039
CRESTON, Paul (b. New York, 1906)
  Symphony No. 2; Symphony No. 3; Mitchell, NASO; (W) WL-5272
DAHL, Ingolf (b. Germany, 1912)
  The Tower of Saint Barbara; Whitney, LO; LOU-56-2
DALLAPICCOLA, Luigi (b. Italy, 1904)
  Canti di Prigionia; Markevitch, SCA; (Angel) 35228
  Tartiniana for Violin and Orchestra; Posselt, Bernstein, orchestra; (C) ML-4996
  Variazioni Per Orchestra; Whitney, LO; LOU-545-8
DEBUSSY, Achille-Claude (b. France, 1862; d. France, 1918)
  Children's Corner; Bergamasque Suite; Gieseking; (A) 35067
  Images pour Orchestre; Monteux, SFSO; (V) LVT-1036

Estampes; Pour le Piano; Images; Gieseking; (A) 35065

Etudes; Gieseking; (A) 35250

Le Martyre de St. Sébastien; soloists, Inghelbrecht, CETO; (DT) DTL-93040/41

La Mer; Nocturnes; Monteux, BSO; (V) LM-1939

Piano Music; Gieseking; (A) 35026

Preludes (Books 1 and 2); Gieseking; (A) 35066, 35249

DELIUS, Frederick (b. England, 1862 (German parents); d. France, 1934)

Appalachia; Koanga; Beecham, RPO; (C) ML-4915

Brigg Fair; On Hearing the First Cuckoo; Song of Summer; Walk to Paradise Garden; Collins, LSO; (L) LL-758

Concerto for Piano; Song of the High Hills; Betty Beecham, Beecham, RPO; (V) LVT-1045

Sea Drift; Boyce, Beecham, BBC Chorus, RPO; (C) ML-5079

DELLO JOIO, Norman (b. New York, 1913)

Triumph of St. Joan Symphony; Whitney, LO; (C) ML-4615

DIAMOND, David (b. Rochester, New York, 1915)

Rounds For Strings; Golschmann, CAO; (CAP) P-8245

EGK, Werner (b. Bavaria, 1901)

French Suite; Geigenmusik; Egk, LEO; (U) C-7022

EINEM, Gottfried von (b. Berne, 1918)

Capriccio for Orchestra, Op. 2; Fricsay, RIAS; (D) DL-9769

ENESCO, Georges (b. Romania, 1881; d.)

Romanian Rhapsodies, Nos. 1, 2, Op. 11; Stokowski, Orch; (V) LM-1878

FALLA, Manuel de (b. Spain, 1876; d. Argentina, 1946)

El Amor Brujo; Merriman, Stokowski, orchestra; (V) LM-1054

Nights in the Gardens of Spain; Novaes, Swarowsky, PMS; (VOX) PL-8520

La Vida Breve; de Los Angeles, soloists, Halffter, BOO; (V) LM-6017

GERSHWIN, George (b. Brooklyn, 1898; d. Hollywood, 1937)

An Amerian In Paris; Bernstein, RCAVS; (V) LM-1803

Concerto in F; Rhapsody in Blue; Sanromá, Fiedler, BPO; (CAM) Cal-304

GINASTERA, Alberto (b. Buenos Aires, 1916)

Pampeana No. 3—A Pastoral Symphony; Whitney, LO; LOU-545-10

Variaciones Concertantes; Dorati, MSO; (M) MG-50047

GLANVILLE-HICKS, Peggy (b. Australia, 1912)

Sonata for piano and Percussion; Concertino da Camera; Bussotti,
NY Percussion Group, NY Woodwind Ensemble; (C) ML-4990
The Transposed Heads; Whitney, KOA, LO; LOU-545-6
GLINKA, Michail Ivanovich (b. Russia, 1804; d. Germany, 1857)
A Life for the Czar; soloists, chorus, Melik-Pashaiev, BTO; (VG)
Vang-6010/12
GOEB, Roger (b. Cherokee, Iowa, 1914)
Quintet for Woodwinds; New Art Wind Quintet; (CE) 2003
Symphony No. 3; Stokowski, Orch; (V) LM-1727
GOULD, Morton (b. Richmond Hill, New York, 1913)
Dance Variations; Stokowski, SFSO; (V) LM-1858
Interplay; Gould, RHDO; (C) ML-4218
GRIFFES, Charles Tomlinson (b. Elmira, N. Y., 1884; d. New York,
1920)
Pleasure Dome of Kubla Khan; The White Peacock; Clouds; Bac-
chanale; Hanson, ERSO; (M) MG-40012
Roman Sketches; Piano Sonata; Hambro; Walden 100
GROFÉ, Ferde (b. New York, 1892)
Grand Canyon Suite; Toscanini, NBCSO; (V) LM-1004
GRUENBERG, Louis (b. Russia, 1884)
Concerto for Violin; Heifetz, Monteux; SFSO; (V) LVT-1017
GUARNIERI, Camargo (b. Tiete, Brazil, 1907)
Suite IV Centenario; Whitney, LO; LOU-56-1
HAIEFF, Alexei (b. Siberia, 1914)
Piano Concerto; Piano Music; Bianca, Smit, Walther, HP; (MGM)
MGM-3243
HANSON, Howard (b. Nebraska, 1896)
Symphony No. 3; Koussevitzky, BSO; (V) LVT-1016
Symphony No. 5 (Sinfonia Sacra); Hanson, ERSO; (M) MG-40014
HARRIS, Roy (b. Lincoln County, Oklahoma, 1898)
Sonata for Violin and Piano; Gingold, J. Harris; (C) ML-4842
Symphony 1933; Symphony No. 7; Ormandy, PO; (C) ML-5095
Symphony No. 3; Koussevitzky, BSO; (V) LVT-1016
HARRISON, Lou (b. Portland, Oregon, 1917)
Suite for Violin, Piano and Small Orchestra; soloists, Stokowsi, or-
chestra; (V) LM-1785
HINDEMITH, Paul (b. Germany, 1895)
Mathis der Maler; Symphonic Dances; Hindemith, BEPO; (D) DL-
9818
Nobilissima Visione; Klemperer, PHO; (A) 35221

Theme and Four Variations; Symphonic Metamorphosis on themes of Weber; Hindemith, BEPO; (D) DL-9829

HIVELY, Wells (b. Corona, California, 1902)

Tres Himnos; Hanson, ERSO; (M) MG-40013

HOLST, Gustav (b. England, 1874; d. London, 1934)

The Planets; Boult, PPO; (W) XWN-18252

HONEGGER, Arthur (b. France, 1892; d. France, 1955 [Swiss citizen])

Jeanne d'arc au Bûcher; Zorina, Lloyd, chorus, Ormandy, PO; (C) SL-178

King David; Honegger, soloists, RFO; (DT) DTL-93004/5

Pacific 231; Rugby; Mouement symphonique No. 3; Prélude pour la tempête; Scherchen, LPSO; (W) LAB-7010

Symphonie Liturgique; Chant de Joie; Denzler, PCO; (L) LL-1296

Symphony No. 5; Munch, BSO; (V) LM-1741

HOVHANESS, Alan (b. Somerville, Massachusetts, 1911)

Concerto No. 1 (Arevakal); Hanson, ERSO; (M) MG-40005

Concerto No. 7 for Orchestra; Whitney, LO; LOU-545-4

The Flowering Peach; Orbit No. 1; Is There Survival; Hovhaness, Chamber Ensemble; (MGM) E-3164

Prelude and Quadruple Fugue; Hanson, ERSO; (M) MG-50106

IBERT, Jacques (b. Paris, 1890)

Divertissement; Slatkin, CAO; (CAP) P-8270

Escales; Paray, DSO; (M) MG-50056

IVES, Charles E. (b. Danbury, Connecticut, 1874)

Four Pieces for Orchestra; Over the Pavements; The Unanswered Question; Hallowe'en; Central Park in the Dark Some Forty Years Ago; Violin Sonata No. 2; Trio: Largo; Cherniavsky, chamber orchestra, various artists; (PO) PRLP-1001

Piano Sonata No. 1; Masselos; (C) ML-4490

Sonata No. 2; J. Kirkpatrick; (C) ML-4250

String Quartet No. 2; Walden String Quartet; (P) SPLP-501

Symphony No. 2; Adler, VO; (SPA) SPA-39

Symphony No. 3; Stewart, BLSO; (V) VRS-468

Three Places in New England; Walter Hendl, ARSO; (ARS) ARS-116

Twenty-Four songs; Boatwright, J. Kirkpatrick; (OV) Over-7

Violin Sonatas I–IV; Druian, Simms; (M) MG-50096/97

JANÁČEK, Leos; (b. Moravia, 1854; d. Prague, 1928)

Concertino; Mladi; Firkusny, ensemble; (C) ML-4995

KAY, Hershy (b. Philadelphia, 1919)
  Western Symphony; Barzin, NYCBO; (VOX) PL-9050
KAY, Ulysses (b. Tucson, 1917)
  Serenade for Orchestra; Whitney, LO; LOU-545-8
KHACHATURIAN, Aram (b. Tiflis, Armenia, 1903)
  Concerto for Piano; Kapell, Koussevitzky, BSO; (V) LM-1006
KIRCHNER, Leon (b. Brooklyn, 1919)
  Quartet No. 1; American Art Quartet; (C) ML-4843
KODÁLY, Zoltán (b. Hungary, 1882)
  Háry János Suite; Rodzinski, PPO; (W) W-LAB-7034
KOHS, Ellis (b. Chicago, 1916)
  Symphony No. 1; Adler, VSO; CRI-104
KŘENEK, Ernst (b. Vienna, 1900)
  Concerto for Violin, Piano, and Orchestra; A. & M. Ajemian, Solo-
    mon, MGMO; (MGM) E-3218
  Eleven Transparencies; Whitney, LO; LOU-56-3
  Pieces for Piano; Sonata No. 3 for Piano, Op. 92, No. 4; Křenek;
    SPA 4
  Sonata No. 4 for Piano; Bagatelles (4) for Piano, 4 hands, Op. 70;
    Abramowitsch, Křenek, Ajemian; (ML) 7014
  Sonata No. 5 for Piano; Zelka; (ML) 7029
  Symphonic Elegy for String Orchestra; Mitropoulos, NYP; (C)
    ML-4524
LIEBERMANN, Rolf (b. Zurich, 1910)
  Concerto for Jazz Band and Orchestra; Reiner, Sauter-Finnegan
    Band, CSO; (V) LM-1888
LOEFFLER, Charles (b. Alsace, 1861; d. Medfield, Massachusetts,
    1935)
  Memories of My Childhood; Poem-La Bonne Chanson; Hanson,
    ERSO; (M) MG-40012
  A Pagan Poem; Rosenthal, PPHO; (CAP) P-8188
LUENING, Otto (b. Milwaukee, 1900)
  Music for Tape Recorder (Sonic Contours, Fantasy In Space, Incan-
    tation, Invention, Low Speed); Ussachevsky, Luening; (I) GB-1
  Rhapsodic Variations for Tape Recorder and Orchestra; Whitney,
    LO; LOU-545-5
McBRIDE, Robert Guyn (b. Tucson, 1911)
  Punch and the Judy; Adler, VO; (CRI) CRI-107
McPHEE, Colin (b. Montreal, 1901)
  Tabuh-Tabuhan; Hanson, ERSO; (M) MG-50103

MALIPIERO, G. Francesco (b. Venice, 1882)
    Rispetti e Strambotti; Stuyvesant Quartet; (PHIL) 101
MARTINU, Bohuslav (b. Czechoslovakia, 1890)
    Concerto; Concerto Grosso; Partita; Serenade; Swoboda, Various
        orchestras; (W) XWN-18079
    Three Madrigals; J. & L. Fuchs; (D) DL-8510
MENNIN, Peter (b. Erie, Pennsylvania, 1923)
    Symphony No. 3; Mitropoulos, NYP; (C) ML-4902
    Symphony No. 6; Whitney, LO; LOU-545-3
MENOTTI, Gian-Carlo (b. Italy, 1911)
    Amahl and the Night Visitors; Original TV Cast; (V) LM 1701
    The Medium; The Telephone; Ballet Society; (C) OSL-154
    Sebastian-Ballet Suite; Stokowski, NBCSO; (V) LM-1858
MILHAUD, Darius (b. France, 1892)
    Le Boeuf sur le Toit; Golschmann, CAO; (CAP) P-8244
    Création du Monde; Bernstein, orchestra; (C) CL-920
    Quartet No. 1 (1912); WQXR Quartet; (PO) PRLP-1004
    Suite Provençale; Golschmann, SSO; (CA) CAL-178
    Symphonies for Small Orchestra, Nos. 1, 2, 3, 5; Milhaud, MMCO;
        (MMS) MMS-108
MOORE, Douglas Stuart (b. Cutchogue, New York, 1893)
    Quintet for Clarinet and Strings; Oppenheim, New Music Quartet;
        (C) ML-4494
    Symphony No. 2; Dixon, ARSO; (ARS) ARS-45
MOROSS, Jerome (b. Brooklyn, 1913)
    Frankie and Johnny; Hendl, ARSO; ARS-12
MOSSOLOV, Alexandre Vassilievich (b. Russia, 1900)
    Iron Foundry; Quadri, LPSO; (W) LAB-7004
MUCZYNSKI, Robert (b. Chicago, 1929)
    Concerto No. 1 For Piano and Orchestra; Whitney, LO; LOU-56-5
MUSSORGSKY, Modest Petrovich (b. Russia, 1839; d. St. Petersburg,
    1881)
    Boris Godounov; Christoff, Gedda, chorus, Dobrowen, RDF; (HMV)
        HMV-6400
    Khovantchina; Baranovich, BNO; (L) XLLA-29
    Night on Bald Mountain; Stokowski, Orch; (V) LM-1816
    The Nursery (Song cycle); Kurenko; (CAP) P-8265
    Orchestral Program; Fair at Sorochinsk (Overture & Gopak); Suss-
        kind, PO; (MGM) E-3030
    Pictures at an Exhibition; Toscanini, NBCSO; (V) LM-1838

Songs and Dances of Death; Tourel, Bernstein, Orch; (C) ML-4289

Sunless Cycle (Songs); Kurenko; (CAP) P-8310

NIELSEN, (August) Carl (b. Denmark, 1865; d. Copenhagen, 1931)

Symphony No. 3, Op. 27 (Sinfonia Espansiva); Frandsen, DNO; (EP) LC-3225

Symphony No. 6 (Sinfonia Semplice); Jensen, DSRO; (M) MG-10137

ORFF, Carl (b. Munich, 1895)

Carmina Burana (Secular Songs); Soloists, chorus, Jochum, BRO; (D) DL-9706

PALMER, Robert (b. Syracuse, New York, 1915)

Quartet for Piano and Strings; Kirkpatrick, Walden Quartet; (C) ML-4842

PERSICHETTI, Vincent (b. Philadelphia, 1915)

Symphony for Strings; Whitney, LO; LOU-545-7

Symphony No. 4, Op. 51; Ormandy, PO; (C) ML-5108

PISTON, Walter (b. Rockland, Maine, 1894)

The Incredible Flutist; Fiedler, BPO; in (V) LM-6113

Symphony No. 3; Hanson, ERSO; (M) MG-40010

Symphony No. 4; Ormandy, PO; (C) ML-4992

PORTER, Quincy (b. New Haven, Connecticut, 1897)

Symphony No. 1; Porter, CCO; (OV) 10

POULENC, Francis (b. Paris, 1899)

Concerto for Two Pianos; Whittemore & Lowe, Mitropoulos, RCAVS; (V) LM-1048

Les Mamelles de Tiresias; Soloists, Chorus, Cluytens, POCO; (Angel) D-35090 or T-35090

Sonata for Two Pianos; Gold & Fizdale; (C) ML-5068

POWELL, John (b. Richmond, 1882)

Rhapsodie Négre; Dixon, ARSO; ARS-20

PROKOFIEV, Sergei (b. Russia, 1891; d. Russia, 1953)

Alexander Nevsky (Cantata, Op. 78); Tourel, choir, Ormandy, PO; (C) ML-4247

Classical Symphony in D Major, Op. 25; Koussevitzky, BSO; (V) LM-1215

Romeo and Juliet, Op. 64; Rozhdestvensky, BTO; (W) XWN-2206

Scythian Suite, Op. 20; Scherchen, VSO; (W) XWN-18266

Sonata No. 2 in D Minor for Piano, Op. 14; Graffman; (V) LM-2012

Sonata No. 7, Op. 83; Horowitz; (V) LM-1016

Symphony No. 5 in B Flat Major, Op. 100; Koussevitzky, BSO; (V) LVT-1026

Violin Concerto No. 1; Piano Concerto No. 3; Oistrakh, Kondrashin, SRO; (W) XWN-18178

RAVEL, Maurice Joseph (b. France, 1875; d. Paris, 1937)

Bolero; Koussevitzky, BSO; (V) LM-1012

Complete Works for Piano Solo; Gieseking; (A) 3541-5S

Concerto for the Left Hand; Casadesus, Ormandy, PO; (C) ML-4075

Quartet in F; Budapest Quartet; (C) ML-4668

Le Tombeau de Couperin; Ansermet, OSR; (L) LL-795

RESPIGHI, Ottorino (b. Italy, 1879; d. Rome, 1936)

Feste Romane; Dorati, MSO; (M) MG-50046

Fountains of Rome; Pines of Rome; Toscanini, NBCSO; (V) LM-1768

REVUELTAS, Silvestre (b. Mexico, 1899)

Cuauhnahuac; Sensemaya; Quadri, LPSO; (W) LAB-7004

RIEGGER, Wallingford (b. Georgia, 1885)

Symphony No. 3; Hanson, ERSO; (C) ML-4902

Variations for Piano and Orchestra; Whitney, LO; LOU-545-3

RIETI, Vittoria (b. Egypt, 1898 [Italian parents])

Partita for Harpsichord; Marlowe, ensemble; (CAP) P-8309

Suite champêtre; Gold, Fizdale; (C) ML-4853

ROGERS, Bernard (b. New York, 1893)

Soliloquy for Flute and Strings; Hanson, ERSO; (M) MG-40003

ROREM, Ned (b. Richmond, Indiana, 1923)

Sonata No. 2 for Piano; Katchen; (L) LL-759

ROSENBERG, Hilding (b. Sweden, 1892)

Louisville Concerto; Whitney, LO; LOU-56-1

Symphony No. 3 (Four Ages of Man); Mann, SRS; (L) LL-944

ROUSSEL, Albert (b. France, 1869; d. France, 1937)

Bacchus et Ariane Suite No. 2, Op. 43; Munch, BSO; (V) LM-1741

Piano Concerto; Concerto for Orchestra; Sinfonietta; Gousseau, Sacher, LAO; (EP) LC-3129

RÓZSA, Miklos (b. Budapest, 1907)

Concerto for Violin; Heifetz, Hendl, DaSO; (V) LM-2027

RUGGLES, Carl (b. Marion, Massachusetts, 1876)

Evocations (4 Chants for Piano); Portals; Men and Mountains

(Lilacs); J. Kirkpatrick, Prausnitz, Juilliard String Orch; (C)
ML-4986

SATIE, Erik-Alfred-Leslie (b. France, 1866; d. Paris, 1925)
Music for Piano; Poulenc; (C) ML-4399; Masselos; (MGM) E-3154
Three Pieces in the Shape of a Pear; R. & G. Casadesus; (C)
ML-4246

SCHÖNBERG, Arnold (b. Vienna, 1874)
Five Pieces for Orchestra, Op. 16; Kubelik, CSO; (M) MG-50024
Gurrelieder; Soloists, Chorus, Liebowitz, ONSS; (HS) HS-100
Pierrot Lunaire; Soloists, Leibowitz, ensemble; (W) WN-18143
Quartets Nos. 1–4 (complete); Juilliard String Quartet; (C) SL-188
Suite, Op. 29; Craft, ensemble; (C) ML-5099
Verklärte Nacht, Op. 4; Stokowski, orchestra; (V) LM-1739
Violin Concerto; Krasner, Mitropoulos, NYP; (C) ML-4857

SCHUMAN, William Howard (b. New York, 1910)
Symphony for Strings; Steinberg, PSO; (CAP) S-8212
Symphony No. 3; Ormandy, PO; (C) ML-4413
Symphony No. 6 (In one movement); Ormandy, PO; (C) ML-4992
Undertow (Choreographic Episodes); Levine, BATO; (CAP) P-
8238

SCRIABIN, Alexander Nikolaievitch (b. Moscow, 1872; d. Moscow,
1915)
Piano Preludes; Horowitz; (V) LM-2005
Poem of Ecstasy, Op. 54; Mitropoulos, NYP; (C) ML-4731

SESSIONS, Roger (b. Brooklyn, 1896)
Black Maskers; Hanson, ERSO; (M) MG-50106
Quartet; Walden Quartet; (C) ML-5104
Symphony No. 2; Mitropoulos, NYP; (C) ML-4784

SHAPERO, Harold (b. Lynn, Massachusetts, 1920)
Credo for Orchestra; Whitney, LO; LOU-56-5
Symphony for Classical Orchestra; Bernstein, orchestra; (C) ML-
4889

SHOSTAKOVICH, Dmitri (b. Russia, 1906)
Quintet, Op. 57; Aller, Hollywood Quartet; (CAP) P-8171
Symphony No. 1 in F Major, Op. 10; Golden Age; Mitchell, NSO;
(W) XWN-18293
Symphony No. 5, Op. 47; Mitropoulos, NYP; (C) ML-4739
Symphony No. 6, Op. 53; Reiner, PSO; (C) ML-4249
Symphony No. 10 in E Minor, Op. 93; Mitropoulos, NYP; (C) ML-
4959

SIBELIUS, Jan (b. Finland, 1865)
  Concerto in D Major for Violin, Op. 47; Symphony No. 3 in C, Op.
    52; Oistrakh, Ehrling, SFO; (A) D-35315 or T-35315
  Quartet in D Minor; Guilet quartet; (CHS) CHS-1092
  Symphony No. 1 in E Minor, Op. 39; Beecham, RPO; (C) ML-4653
  Symphony No. 2 in D Major, Op. 43; Koussevitzky, BSO; (V)
    LM-1172
  Symphony No. 4 in A Minor, Op. 63; Ehrling, SRSO; (M) MG-
    10143
  Symphony No. 5 in E Flat Major, Op. 82; Symphony No. 7 in C
    Major, Op. 105; Koussevitzky, BSO, BBC; (V) LVT-1015
SIEGMEISTER, Elie (b. New York, 1909)
  Ozark Set; Walther, HP; (MGM) E-3141
SMETANA, Bedřich (b. Bohemia, 1824; d. Prague, 1884)
  The Bartered Bride; Soloists, chorus, Vogel, PNTO; (U) URLP-231
SOWERBY, Leo (b. Grand Rapids, 1895)
  Symphony for Organ in G; Crozier; (Ken) 2554
STEVENS, Halsey (b. Scott, New York, 1908)
  Triskelion; Whitney, LO; LOU-545-1
STILL, William Grant (b. Mississippi, 1895)
  Afro-American Symphony (and Piano Pieces); Krueger, VOO;
    (NR) 105
STRAUSS, Richard (b. Munich, 1864; d. Garmisch, 1949)
  Alpine Symphony, Op. 64; Konwitschny, MUOO; (Ur) A-7064
  Also Sprach Zarathustra, Op. 30; Reiner, CSO; (V) LM-1806
  Arabella; Soloists, von Matacic; PHO; (Angel) 35194
  Ariadne auf Naxos; Soloists, von Karajan, PHO; (Angel) 3532
  Capriccio; Soloists, Ackermann, PHO; (Angel) 35084
  Death and Transfiguration, Op. 24; Till Eulenspiegel; Toscanini,
    NBCSO: (V) LM-1891
  Don Juan, Op. 20; Reiner, CSO; (V) LM-1888
  Don Quixote, Op. 35; Piatigorsky, Munch, BSO; (V) LM-1781
  Heldenleben, Ein, Op. 40; Reiner, CSO; (V) LM-1807
  Der Rosenkavalier; Soloists, Kleiber, VPO; (L) XLLA-22
  Salome; Elektra; Bourgeois Gentilhomme; Soloists, Reiner, CSO; (V)
    LM-6047
STRAVINSKY, Igor Feodorovich (b. Russia, 1882)
  Baiser de la Fée; Stravinsky, CO; (C) ML-5102
  Firebird Suite; Le Sacre du Printemps; Stravinsky, NYP; (C)
    ML-4882

L'Histoire du Soldat Suite; Octet; Symphonies of Wind Instruments;
Stravinsky, various ensembles; (C) ML-4964

Oedipus Rex; Chorus, Stravinsky, CRSO; (C) ML-4644

The Rake's Progress; Soloists, Stravinsky, MOO; (C) SL-125

Symphony in C; Cantata; Soloists, choir, ensemble, Stravinsky, CO;
(C) ML-4899

Symphony In Three Movements; Symphony of Psalms; Stravinsky,
NYP; Chorus, CBSS; (C) ML-4129

SWANSON, Howard (b. Atlanta, 1909)
Short Symphony; Litschauer, VSOO; (VG) VRS-434

TANSMAN, Alexander (b. Poland, 1897)
Triptych; ZS; (D) DL-9625

THOMPSON, Randall (b. New York, 1899)
Symphony No. 2 in E Minor; Dixon, ARSO; (ARS) ARS-45
The Testament of Freedom; Chorus, Hanson, ERSO; (M) MG-40000

THOMSON, Virgil (b. Kansas City, 1896)
Filling Station; Barzin, NYCBO; (VOX) PL-9050
Four Saints In Three Acts; Thomson, soloists, chorus, orchestra;
(V) LCT-1139
The Mother of Us All Suite; Janssen; JSLA; (C) ML-4468
Quartet No. 2; Juilliard Quartet; (C) ML-4987
Three Pictures for Orchestra; Songs; Thomson, PO; (C) ML-4919

USSACHEVSKY, Vladimir (b. China, 1911) See Luening

VARÈSE, Edgar (b. Paris, 1885)
Density 21.5; Integrales; Ionization; Octandre; LeRoy, ensembles;
(EMS) EMS-401

VAUGHAN WILLIAMS, Ralph (b. England, 1872)
Fantasia on a Theme by Tallis; Greensleeves; Boult, PPO; (W) WL-7048
Symphony No. 2 (London); Boult, LPO; (L) LL-569
Symphony No. 4 in F Minor; Boult, LPO; (L) LL-974
Symphony No. 5 in D Major; Boult, LPO; (L) LL-975
Symphony No. 6 in E Minor; Stokowski, NYP; (C) ML-4214
Symphony No. 8; Barbirolli, HO; (M) MG-50115

VILLA-LOBOS, Heitor (b. Rio de Janeiro, 1881)
Bachianas Brasileiras No. 1; Marx, BFO; (V) LCT-1143
Bachianas Brasileiras No. 5; Sayao; (C) AAL-3
Dawn In A Tropical Forest; Whitney, LO; LOU-545-1
Quatuor; Nonetto; Roger Wagner Chorale; (CAP) P-8191

WALTON, William (b. England, 1902)
  Concerto for Violin and Orchestra; Heifetz, Walton, PHO; (V) LM-1121
  Façade; Sitwell, Pears, Collins, EOE; (L) LL-1133
WARD, Robert (b. Cleveland, 1917)
  Symphony No. 3; Johnson, CISO; (R) 199–185
WEBER, Ben (b. St. Louis, 1916)
  Prelude and Passacaglia, Op. 42; Whitney, LO; LOU-56-6
  Symphony on Poems of William Blake, Op. 33; Galjour, Stokowski, orchestra; (V) LM-1785
WEBERN, Anton von (b. Vienna, 1883; d. Austria, 1945)
  Five Movements for String Quartet; Juilliard Quartet; (C) ML-4737
WEILL, Kurt (b. Germany, 1900; d. New York, 1950)
  Concerto for Violin & Wind Orchestra, Op. 12; Ajemian, Solomon, ensemble; (MGM) E-3179
  The Threepenny Opera; Lenya, Merrill, Wolfson, Sullivan; (MGM) E-3121
WOLPE, Stepan (b. New York, 1924)
  Passacaglia; Percussion Quartet; Sonata for Violin and Piano; Tudor, Magnes, Baron, ensemble; (ES) 530

INDEX